Follow the Leaders

Successful Trading Techniques with Line Drive Stocks

RICHARD BLACKMAN

Simon and Schuster
New York

Designed by Irving Perkins
Manufactured in the United States of America

Library of Congress Cataloging in Publication Data
Blackman, Richard.
      Follow the leaders.
      Bibliography: p.
      1. Speculation. 2. Stocks. I. Title.
HG6041.B56   332.6′45   77–10954
            ISBN 0-671-22471-9

Contents

*To my wife, Elayne,
and our daughters,
Lisa and Laura*

FOREWORD

Of the hundreds of books written about investments and the stock market, only a handful have met the test of time: Benjamin Graham's *The Intelligent Investor* and *Security Analysis,* Burton Crane's *The Sophisticated Investor* and Gerald Loeb's *Battle* books. They have continued to be popular because they provide useful information in an understandable manner.

I believe *Follow the Leaders* will join these perennial favorites. In down-to-earth language and with real-life examples, Richard Blackman explains how to use charts to discover what major investors are doing, and, most important, how to reduce a loss or retain profits by timely selling. As most of us have learned by experience, investment success relies as much on minimizing losses as on maximizing profits.

At first, I found it difficult to accept the Blackman discipline and rules. But I soon realized the wisdom of his insistence on investing only in UP stocks in UP groups in UP markets. From personal experience, I am persuaded that Blackman Strategy points the way to doubling the value of your investment portfolio every year!

Follow the Leaders is a must book for:

(1) Every investor who really wants to make money in the stock market;

(2) All registered representatives who are genuinely concerned in helping their clients;

(3) Most professionals who are responsible for the wise, conservative and profitable management of fiduciary funds.

9

Even if you do not agree with all of Blackman's advice, this book can make you a better investor.

C. COLBURN HARDY
East Orange, N.J.   July 1977

C. Colburn Hardy is editor of Dun & Bradstreet's *Your Investments* and author of eight books on investments and personal money management.

1. How to Make Money in the Stock Market by Following Institutional Investors

There's only one reason to invest: *to make money*. That means to use your capital to achieve the greatest rewards in the shortest time with the least risks. Income is welcome, but in the stock market, really worthwhile returns can be gained only by capital appreciation: by a rise in the value of the securities you own.

I believe that the best and surest way to make money with stocks is to *follow the leaders:* (1) the big institutional investors who dominate the trading on the New York Stock Exchange (NYSE) and thus determine the supply and demand for widely owned securities; (2) the major corporations whose shares are considered suitable investments for professionally managed portfolios. These companies are leaders in their industries. Many of their names are household words. Yet at any one time, only about 400 will meet the institutional standards of quality and value.

When the Big Boys start to buy heavily (tens of thousands of shares), the prices of these quality stocks are almost sure to go up. When they sell, the market values of these same stocks will go down.

This book will show you how to catch these moves and make high profits and to take small losses. With Blackman Strategy, you don't have to fret over decisions. You deal only with quality issues and act only after the experts have started to make their moves. When there are no immediate prospects for substantial gains, you get out of the market and keep your money in a savings account.

The goal of my theories is to show you how to turn $5,000 into $50,000 or to make $50,000 grow to $300,000. *And to keep those profits.*

With this extra money, even after paying taxes, you will be able to

11

change your life style. Or if you are older, this nest egg will make it possible for you and your spouse to do most everything you've ever dreamed of. I firmly believe that anyone with modest savings can achieve financial independence by following the principles and practices explained in this book.

Success is sure but not easy. It requires discipline, patience and realism—the ability to deal with things as they are, not as you would like them to be.

In many areas, this is a book of contrary opinion. It exposes some Wall Street investment myths and the hypocrisy of the pontifications of security analysts, brokers and investment advisers. Yet, the book has a positive motif and sets forth specific guidelines that can help you to make money with your savings.

This book was written for the individual investor, not for the professional who handles millions of dollars of fiduciary funds. These big money managers can afford to hold stocks for years and forget about temporary fluctuations. They rely on the growth of America and so they often pay little attention to timing purchases or sales (one reason why professional investment results have been so poor). Still, I believe that such long-term investors can improve their total returns by following the theories and techniques explained here.

IMPORTANCE OF SMART SELLING

This is a *sell* book. It is quite different from most investment advice that stresses *buying* and how to locate stocks which will increase in value over the years. Most advisers, and all brokers, are "good" at telling you what to buy, but are silent or, at least, fuzzy about selling. Once they make a recommendation, they tell you to hang on no matter what happens to the stock. Too often, you are the one who has to make the decision to sell, and then usually when you have a substantial loss.

I believe that one of the most important factors in successful investing is knowing when to sell. With my theories, you can learn how to do this to keep your losses small and to let your profits run.

IDEAS THAT WORK

In the pages that follow, you will discover the strategies that are used by the true professionals: the handful of men and women who really profit from their investments in securities.

These ideas are based on my 17 years of hard-nosed experience in Wall Street: from trainee in a major brokerage firm to chairman of a multimillion-dollar corporation. What I say will not be popular with registered representatives (RRs). Many of my concepts are counter to the traditional counsel and practices that have proven profitable for brokers and, usually, disastrous for individual investors.

These theories work. They provide high returns in all kinds of stock markets and are especially valuable in bull markets, which, I am confident, will come in the years ahead.

Most people have been taught in classes and seminars, in articles and books, by parents and friends, by brokers and bankers, that:

1. Money should be invested for the long term in a diversified group of securities

2. Trading is only for speculators

3. The greatest financial rewards involve the greatest risks

4. Buy low and sell high

5. Get into a stock early and hold for appreciation even if this takes years

6. The small investor can never hope to compete successfully with the professionals

I disagree, in whole or part, with every one of these shibboleths. That's why this book will show you how to take advantage of those misconceptions and use tactics that will assure profits greater than those achieved by most brokers and investment advisers and far greater than those of the majority of individual investors.

My basic concepts are simple:

1. *Follow the leaders.* Over two thirds of all transactions of stocks listed on the New York Stock Exchange (NYSE) are made by institutional investors (investment companies, trust departments, banks, investment advisers and insurance companies) and NYSE member firms for their own accounts. Generally their decisions to buy or sell are based on in-depth research supplemented by information not readily available to the general public.

By the time this special knowledge reaches the individual investor, through research reports or financial news, the Big Boys have already made their moves. Much of Blackman Strategy is based on my belief that everyone who invests his savings in the stock market can be successful by following these leaders.

2. *Professional decisions to buy or sell represent what informed investors anticipate will happen in the near future.* This concept is closely related to the established fact that the stock market forecasts the economy.

With few exceptions, a rise or fall in the price of the stock of a major corporation reflects conditions which will not be known publicly or become effective for another six months or so.

3. *Every major move in every listed stock is shown by charts.* These

graphic reports record the trends resulting from supply and demand: *up* when major investors start to buy; *down* when they begin to sell. By following charts and reacting to their signals, you can use the decisions of professional money managers for personal financial benefit.

From long experience, I have learned that:

(a) Charts tell the truth and reveal the winners and losers;

(b) More profits are made by not buying losers than by owning winners.

I *always* sell when the chart trendline breaks on the downside even if the sale is only a day or two after my purchase.

I *always* sell when a stock starts to lose its upward momentum and moves sideways. Such going-nowhere action indicates that demand is dwindling and there is small chance for a rise and a large probability of a decline.

4. *A trend will continue in the same direction until something important forces a change.* Remember your high school physics: When you throw a ball, it goes straight until the velocity diminishes and the pull of gravity becomes dominant or the ball meets another object.

This principle applies to the stock market generally and to individual stocks specifically. The trends are always identifiable on charts.

By using charts, I buy high and sell higher. I know that the best profits come from an *up* stock in an *up* group in an *up* market.

I look for a line-drive stock: one that can move almost straight up, with few corrections, for a gain of 20 percent or more. This is the time when the institutions work for me. I try to think as they do and to watch the charts to see how vigorously the professionals are buying. When the timing is right, I use my purchases to keep the trend moving upward.

5. *Trading is the key to success in the stock market.* By this, I mean informed trading that follows the patterns set by major investors. These can be seen on charts. When I find a line-drive *up* stock, I buy and trade—selling when it hits the top of its channel; buying when there's a temporary dip to the bottom of the channel. I may hold a stock only a few hours, or for months. At all times, I hold it only when I am making money or see such a possibility soon.

6. *The only stocks to own are quality issues which are on the lists of institutional investors.* The risks are small and the potential rewards great. Stocks of marginal or little-known companies will seldom be attractive to big buyers.

7. *Concentration of investments is essential.* Put your money where the action is. Diversification lessens gains and increases risks. When I have a winner, I keep buying as long as there is an *up* trend. With Blackman Strategy, the greatest profits are made by owning one or two stocks at a time.

This concentration enables me to profit from institutional action because these professionals invest as a herd. They follow their own leaders. Demand encourages more demand and ever-higher stock prices. Vice versa when it comes to selling.

If you can make a 20 percent profit on your total capital three times a year (my goal and my record), you will be vastly richer than if you show an average annual total return of 15 percent, which is half again better than achieved by most individual investors, and double the record of institutions.

8. *When you can't make money in the stock market, get out.* Put your savings in the bank and draw daily interest. You can be fully invested all the way to the poorhouse.

There's no reason to risk your wealth when there are no realistic opportunities for worthwhile profits. In a typical year, I may be in the market only three or four times.

Only the foolish listen to selfish brokers who want everyone to keep their money invested in securities at all times and under all conditions. Over a three-to-six-months' period, the 5½ percent return from your thrift account is as profitable as the after-commissions income from Treasury bills or bonds. And you are always liquid and ready to move fast when you find a new potential winner.

9. *Discipline is the single most important factor in success in the stock market.* You must learn to act on chart action and forget predictions, projections and forecasts except as background. Never fight the tape even when you are personally convinced that the market action is wrong or illogical.

10. *Technical analysis is one of the most important tools in successful investing.* It shows what the stock market is doing, not what you think it should do. Charts do not work every time, but they work most of the time: at least seven out of every ten actions signal the direction of the stock and an even higher percentage show the direction of the stock market.

MY OWN RECORD

There can be no guarantee of success in any kind of investment, but I've done well over the years. I am not afraid to show my clients my bank account where my trading dollars are held when I'm out of the market. I've made mistakes, but the profitable trades have been greater, in numbers and dollars, than those resulting in losses.

Experience has helped me to refine my theories and practice. I've made more money over the years and, more important, so have my customers, when they followed my advice. My lifestyle reflects not only W-2 form income from business, but also the benefits of capital accumulated from stock market gains.

I found, however, that as my firm moved into a wider area, there were more skeptics. New customers, and some of the old, refused to believe that any strategy could continue to assure such welcome returns.

In January 1975, I decided that, as the boss man of a small brokerage firm, I had a responsibility to prove my belief that the small investor, using a sane, disciplined program, could make solid profits and, by employing equally sound selling techniques, could keep those hard-won gains.

The market was strong and appeared to be still growing muscle. It seemed to me that this was an unusual opportunity to make a killing and to prove the validity of my theories. That's when I set up a Laboratory Account.

The details are described later. I started with stock and cash worth a little over $1,500. Six months later, with the help of some quickly replaced reserve funds, the account had grown to over $18,000. Even assuming that I had paid full commissions, the account would have been worth almost $15,000.

Here was proof that Blackman Strategy worked. You can do as well with a little experience, a good broker and the rules explained in this book:

1. Hold all cash at least 20 percent of the time

2. Follow the leaders: know what institutions are thinking

3. Act promptly on technical/chart signals: buy on the uptrend; sell when the charts point to a downmove in the stock or the market

4. Be willing to sell and take a small, fast loss

5. Stay liquid enough to take advantage of a line-drive stock when you find one

These rules are not a get-rich-quick scheme. They comprise a solid, market-tested, reliable, sensible route to stock market profits.

Now let's get down to some of the fundamentals and learn the background for this money-making investment strategy.

2.   Why I Wrote This Book

I wrote this book because I am convinced that the small individual investor has not been told the truth about the stock market. In fact, I believe that he has been manipulated, ignored and so misinformed that he has lost not only money but confidence in Wall Street.

Yet I am convinced that everyone should understand the profit-making power of securities, especially common stocks. And I am equally sure that anyone who will follow the guidelines of this book can make money with his/her investments in all kinds of markets.

The idea of writing this book started in late September 1974. We were still in a brutal bear market of incredible stamina, nearly four years old. Statistics indicated that Wall Street was in almost as bad shape as it had been in the 1930s.

For some time, I had been wondering about my profession and my own career. I sat down and took a long look at the past and reviewed the probable future. I had been in the brokerage business since 1960, and for the last five years had been chairman of a member firm of the New York Stock Exchange. Although I was responsible for a multimillion-dollar operation, I still continued to work as a registered representative handling individual accounts. I thought, "Who else does what I do? And with such success? Who works as chief executive officer of a busy brokerage house and also handles small accounts, trading for them on a day-to-day basis?"

There may be others, but they are few and I do not know them.

What worried me was that Wall Street was giving lip service to individual investors but concentrating most of its efforts on the large institutions. Instead of trying to help the small investor, most brokerage firms were hurting him by raising commissions on small lots, by perpetuating false myths, by palming off useless research and by encouraging double standards: advising

17

individuals to avoid the very tactics which the firm's professionals were using profitably.

On the positive side, I realized that I had been handling retail accounts throughout my entire career and, from personal and client experience, I knew the strategies and techniques that worked for small investors.

OUTMODED PRACTICES

When I started in Wall Street in 1960, being a stock broker was a respected, interesting, creative occupation. I was proud to be part of this important financial community. By the early 1970s, the broker was an endangered species. Scores of member firms and hundreds of offices were out of business, either voluntarily or through merger or bankruptcy. Six of every ten registered representatives were looking for work, and many of those who had a job wondered if they would be employed tomorrow. Yet the survivors were still quoting the same old garbage and following the same outmoded theories and practices that had brought on these disasters.

From my contacts, I saw that too many Wall Street firms were becoming hand-holders to wealthy coupon-clippers who were playing golf and vacationing. The large brokers had become involved primarily with huge moneyed interests: giant corporations, banks and trust companies and institutional investors—all groups that controlled billions of dollars. The role of the individual investor (who, I had always thought, was the basis of the stock exchange) was lessening. Anyone who had $5,000 to $100,000 was being given a runaround and a fleecing that put a snake-oil salesman to shame.

When brokerage services were unbundled, and negotiated rates became legal on May 1, 1975, the commissions to big buyers dropped by as much as 50 percent and, later, to 90 percent of the previous charges. But with the super-large wire houses leading the way, the commission for trading 100 to 200 shares was boosted by as much as 50 percent, and in most cases has been maintained at this high level.

This was a crunching blow to the little man. It was proof that these big firms, regardless of their advertising claims, didn't give a damn for the small, individual investor and cared even less whether he made or lost money.

From personal experience, I knew that these higher fees were being used to recoup the costs of management mistakes such as idiotic overexpansion. The small investor paid for new retail offices and the firm's entry into big-money areas such as investment banking, underwriting and fiduciary fund management. With many large brokers, retail offices were no longer sources of investment advice and customer service but were primarily distribution centers for security offerings.

The research rip-off is even more one-sided. The voluminous analyses and detailed reports are designed to woo the institutions. The information seldom gets to the small investor, and when it does, it is almost worthless.

During the long bear market, most research heads of large firms were interested in only one thing: protecting their $40,000 to $80,000 (and up) jobs. They never came out with honest advice: "Go into cash or sell short." They kept making buy recommendations to create commissions for registered reps, not to achieve profits for the unsophisticated investor. They were aware that it's easier to persuade a poorly informed customer to buy than to sell short or take his/her money out of the stock market.

IMPORTANCE OF SHORT SELLING

Yet they knew, as did other firm executives, that in a bear market, short selling is one of the few ways to make money. They also knew that the professionals were taking short positions with their own money. Yet, time and again, the only advice was: "Going short is too risky, un-American, only for speculators."

The truth is that short selling was the only way our firm survived! Black Stein Kimball, Inc., was formed in 1970, just before one of the worst economic periods in American history. Until the bear market bottomed four years later, we concentrated on selling short, with considerable success, for ourselves and for many of our customers.

This experience taught me the power of Wall Street myths. Many of our retail customers refused to go short even though common sense told them that this was the technique to use at the time. If the market is going down, why not profit by this trend? In a free market, stocks are bound to go down sooner or later because our economy runs in cycles. There are periods of growth, then periods of recession. The wise investor uses this knowledge.

In talking with our customers, we found that there were two reasons why they refused to sell short: (1) Fear of the unknown; (2) Ignorance of the registered representatives with whom they had dealt in the past. Further checking convinced us that *most brokers have never sold short in their lives!*

This was the background for one of our most successful programs: on-the-job training for our customers on how to make money in down markets.

CONVICTIONS PAY OFF

At the outset we had a limited clientele, but when they saw the profits that could be made, they increased their short selling and told their friends. BSK survived and prospered because we told the truth and had the courage of our convictions.

This unwillingness of Wall Street to face facts and provide honest advice points up the contradictions that are always at work within the investment community:

• In one firm, you will find meticulously ethical, honest people. Next door are some of the coldest rip-off artists in the entire business world.

• In the same organization, you can meet calm, intelligent, concerned men and women who believe in obeying rules and giving their customers honest (though often misguided) opinions. In the next office will be short-sighted, supercilious fools who seem to base their analyses on reading tea leaves, and who feel no qualms when they thrust this "advice" on the gullible public.

The so-called investment advisers are just as bad. Their recommendations are usually stupid, often hysterical and almost always wrong: "Buy gold at any price . . . Pack a cabin in Canada with canned goods before it's too late . . . Gloom and doom . . . The dollar is dying . . . Capitalism is dead . . . The Dow will drop below 500."

No wonder the individual investor is slow to come back into the market! He is intelligent enough to want advice that makes sense and can be used to achieve profits, not to increase losses.

It seems to me that the problem with most of these "experts," whether columnists, authors, magazine writers, analysts or advisers, is that they have never handled individual accounts. They do not understand the hopes, dreams and fears of individual investors who want to make their savings grow. They have no idea of what it's like to risk hard-earned money. They do not grasp the basic goal of all investing: TO MAKE MONEY.

CONTRARY OPINION

In October 1974, there were clear signs that the bull market was on its way. Most of the advisory services were still recommending that you buy gold and get your snowshoes restrung to hike away from the Wall Street disaster and hole up in Canada. But I was ready to make money.

The background was good. The world situation was becoming more stable. The long, debilitating, nightmarish Vietnam war was behind us. Old money from Europe and new money from the Middle East were flowing into the United States. As I saw it, this was an ideal time for the small investor to score in the stock market, and for me and my firm to make money.

This led me to define who should be in the stock market. Basically, I believe that everyone who is willing to work hard, to accept discipline and to use his/her common sense can make savings grow through investment in securities. This includes millions of Americans who have been scared off because of Wall Street's tired advice and ridiculous myths from the age of J. P. Morgan. These are the people who are too smart to accept the false shibboleths: "Maintain large insurance"; Pile up cash in the bank"; and, if you do become brave enough to risk your savings, "Invest only for the long term."

These concepts may have some merit for some people on some occasions, but it is absurd advice in a bull market when prices are going up.

To my mind, investors can be divided into three groups:

1. The fools who read the rules of the game but do not follow them. They lose money most of the time and only profit from lucky choices

2. The uninformed who do not know the rules and so cannot be expected to follow them

3. The winners: those few individuals who know the rules and who follow them

Obviously, you want to be in (3). That's the basis for the Blackman Strategy.

As you will find out for yourself, you cannot rely on luck in the stock market. You have to learn the rules and follow them absolutely. Ignorance may get you sympathy, but only knowledge and discipline will assure profits.

Most important: You must forget the old advice of Wall Street; you must recognize that with taxes and inflation, bank interest will just about keep pace with the decline in purchasing power; and you must be anxious to make your money grow. Dabbling will never be successful over the long term.

WHAT TRIGGERED THIS BOOK

The actual writing of *Follow the Leaders* was the result of a meeting with two people who wanted to start an investment program. I realized there was a need for a book to correct their misunderstanding and overcome their timidity. It happened like this:

In the spring of 1975, a young couple walked into our office to ask about buying stocks as part of their financial planning. They were typical of many noninvestors who make a good living but want more money for a better life now and greater security in the future.

The husband was a branch manager of a major bank; the wife was a scientist with a large international corporation. They lived in an apartment, had no children, earned a total of $50,000 a year, paid substantial taxes and had savings of $21,300. He owned 100 shares of stock in his bank and she was buying stock in her company through a matched savings plan.

I told them they were in excellent financial condition and, at their ages, were making a wise decision to invest in securities. I suggested growth stocks. They agreed, as long as the selections were strong, quality companies like IBM or Eastman Kodak.

This gave me the opportunity to explain my theory of concentrating on the best stocks to increase capital. "And," I added, "our firm will be happy to do business with you."

Then I asked how much money they would like to invest. Their answer: "$2,000."

This was so unrealistic that I asked them to explain why they had reached such a decision and how they expected such a small portion of their savings to help them achieve their financial goals.

As they talked, I realized that this young couple were among "the uninformed" mentioned earlier. They had been listening to outmoded advice that paid no attention to the realities of the present stock market or of their own hopes. The sum they had in mind to invest left no room for maneuvering: that is, buying quality stocks and trading up when the time was ripe.

Knowing that they were intelligent people, I asked them if they would be willing to spend a little time to let me explain my theories and learn why I was convinced they were sound, practical and rewarding.

That talk became the basis for this book. And, I am happy to say, the young couple did increase their investment, and in the next few months they made substantial profits.

3. Two Kinds of Stocks, Two Kinds of Markets

It may sound simplistic, but the truth is that there are only two types of stocks and two types of markets: UP stocks and DOWN stocks; UP markets and DOWN markets. People who need complexity in their economic lives will reject this statement as being naïve. Yet, in my experience, these are the same individuals who lose money in the stock market.

I've had many an argument about this concept with fundamentalists, technicians and even some clients. Almost all of them insist that there's another type of market: the "sideways" market, which is defined as "an intermediate correction in a strong UP market."

Well, they remind me of romantics seeking unicorns. It's a hopeless quest. Like the fabled unicorn, "sideways markets" do not exist. The title may sound impressive and descriptive, but, to my mind, it's just a fancy name for a DOWN market. Depending on the stock, such lateral movements can cost you a lot of money: a loss of 10 to 20 percent plus the failure to make a profit with that money if you had sold when the trend was no longer up.

Under the Blackman Strategy, there are four basic rules, all keyed to UP stocks and, usually to UP markets. They are:

1. Buy UP
2. Deal with facts, not hopes
3. Insist on quality
4. Follow the leaders

Buy Up. As will be repeated throughout this book, I believe that the time to buy is when the stock market is rising. When the market is not going up (and that includes sideways movements), do *not* purchase stocks. Hold cash. Put your money in a savings account. Wait for profitable buying opportunities.

When there's a bear market, consider selling short. Generally, this technique should be used only in deep market declines. This is the only time to pay attention to DOWN stocks.

Following this rule, it stands to reason that you should purchase only UP stocks: those which have already moved ahead but still have prospects of a continuing rise.

There's no mystery about discovering UP stocks. Let technical analysis be your detective. Rely primarily on charts, but do not neglect other signals.

Deal with Facts, Not Hopes. Throughout my years in Wall Street, I have heard the same story time and again. Unfortunately, I expect to hear it repeated. It's always the same: hopes, dreams, euphoria—all of which, to my mind, add up to *nonsense*.

"I like ABC stock because they are coming out with a new product."

"I like PDQ because I heard the earnings will be turning around next year."

"I like XYZ because my brother-in-law has an 'in' and says sales are going to be way up next year."

If you want to make money in the stock market, ignore every one of these familiar phrases and concentrate on Rule Number 2, which, in full form, is:

Deal with Things as They Are, Not as You Would Like Them to Be. The stock market is a battle for survival. Unless you have money to burn, there is no room for dreams. You must be realistic at all times. Do not speculate on hopes.

Look to your charts. Discover for yourself whether or not you are considering true UP stocks or just kidding yourself, or, worse, being kidded by your broker.

For my own account, and for as many customers as will accept my advice, I purchase UP stocks 90 percent of the time. I look for issues where the technical patterns clearly show that the stocks are climbing.

If you're traveling in the stock market, catch an express train. Ignore the scenery. Get to your destination with a minimum of effort and a maximum of speed. Grab those first-class, no-nonsense UP stocks: those which important investors are spending millions of dollars to acquire. Never mind why. Just follow their lead.

Insist on Quality. When I said "first class," I meant the type of stocks you should buy: the highest quality equities—the deep blue chips that are suitable for institutional portfolios.

If you can make money trading General Motors, why waste your capital on shares of North Dakota Widget Manufacturing?

With few exceptions (and only on solid facts), buy only stocks rated B+ or higher by Standard & Poor's (see Chapter 9). When you spot an UP stock, check its quality before spending any time on further analysis. With low-ranked stocks, the risks almost always outweigh the potential rewards. By concentrating your money in quality stocks, you can gain both security and rewarding profits.

Follow the Leaders. By that, I mean use the Big Boys to make money for yourself. Take advantage of their research, their decisions and their trading techniques. Ignorance of their methods can be costly and may be destructive.

In listing stock ownership, S&P's Stock Guide defines institutions as "Financial institutions—investment and insurance companies." These are only part of the real group that is so important in the stock market. In Wall Street terms, the list should add such other big money investors as trust departments, pension funds, foundations, and thrift institutions.

Their investment resources are huge. In 1974, assets under bank trust management totaled $171 billion. Of this, an estimated $86 billion were handled by six New York City banks.

Mutual funds manage another $46 billion; life insurance companies $22 billion; and foundations, $18 billion. In most cases, their assets are growing rapidly with ever higher contributions to corporate and personal pension funds and profit-sharing plans.

These institutions are a tremendous force in the stock market. In a 1974 study, they accounted for over half of all trading on the New York Stock Exchange. They will continue to be ever more dominant:

TRANSACTIONS ON THE NEW YORK STOCK EXCHANGE

	1969	1974	1980 (estimated)
Institutions	46%	51%	55%
Member firms	25	26	25
Individuals	29	23	20

This is not so awesome as it appears. The bigger the institutions, the more predictable they become. As this book will explain, their actions can be used by the individual investor to spot trends and improve timing of buying and selling.

The Big Boys have a powerful influence on the action of specific stocks. In 1975, the trust department of Morgan Guaranty Trust Company bought 30 percent of all shares of Inco, Ltd., and 28.5 percent of the common stock of Crown Zellerbach Corporation.

In selecting common stock for their portfolios, these professional money managers concentrate on a small number of corporations: at any one time, no more than one quarter of the 1,600 common stocks listed on the Big Board.

The "OK to Buy" list is even smaller: about 50 stocks for a $500 million assets institution. Each of these stocks is carefully selected from a longer list of major companies which have been subject to painstaking fundamental and technical analysis. In most cases, the portfolio manager must get approval from an investment committee which insists on: (1) quality (the financial strength and long-term record of profitable growth of the company); (2) value (which spotlights the price range at which a stock should be bought or sold). The selection standards are high. Generally, they require that fundamental analysis indicates the probability that corporate earnings will be up at least 10 percent in the next 12 months and even more in five years.

THE HERD INSTINCT

Because of the limitation on the number of stocks and the insistence on quality, the Buy lists do not vary a great deal. A comparison of the 50 major holdings of pension funds managed by New York banks and those directed by insurance companies showed 37 of the same equities! As a result of this uniformity, institutions tend to invest as a herd. *They follow their leaders.*

Let's say that on Institution X's Buy List, nine of the 50 stocks are those of drug companies. At lunch, the portfolio manager tells his friend, manager of Institution Y, "The drugs are really looking good to me."

That afternoon, Y's manager starts checking the drug group. He likes what he sees and, after further review, starts to put his fund's money into Merck, Upjohn, Warner-Lambert, etc.

Institution Z's manager hears a rumor (and rumors spread faster in Wall Street than anywhere in the world), notes the market activity in the drug group and decides he doesn't want to be left behind. The stampede is on. Suddenly the drug stocks boom.

On the charts, this concentration of capital shows the start of a line drive: quick, straight up and, with almost no correction, a gain of at least 20 percent. Now these are UP stocks in an UP group, and they showed up in "technical analyses."

This is the time to let the institutions work for you. You do not have to tape-record luncheon conversations or get an "inside" tip. All you—and your broker—have to do is to watch the charts. Then join in with a sizable investment in one or more of these line-drive drug stocks in what is now a line-drive industry.

Actually you can beat the institutions at their own game. As a small investor, you can use your liquidity to get in and out precisely when you want.

To score the Big Hit, follow the leaders. This is what the successful trader looks for. You won't find a line-drive situation every day or even every month. Be patient. By waiting for the right signal revealed by the charts, and by concentrating your capital in quality stocks that are moving UP, you will have the beginning of a sensible, professional stock market strategy.

4. The Importance of Technical Analysis

The goal of both fundamental and technical analysis is the same: to identify those stocks which are most likely to advance in price or, when you are planning to sell short, those most likely to decline. These two types of analysis should not conflict. They approach the same problem from different, though related, points of view.

Fundamental analysis considers the material facts about a corporation: its financial strength, record of profitability and growth, future prospects for the industry and company, etc. From these data, the fundamentalist attempts to arrive at a logical value for the stock, and then compares this with its current and anticipated price. Such basic research always measures the quality of the corporation.

Technical analysis assumes that all of these fundamentals have been taken into account and are being reflected in the market action of the stock. The technician attempts to project a logical evaluation of the present and future price of a stock by watching indexes, primarily charts. Technical analysis is a tool to increase investment accuracy and timing. In my experience, when properly interpreted, technical analysis is correct 80 percent of the time.

I believe that both types of investment analysis can, and should be, combined to assure the greatest profits in the stock market. But I am also convinced that when there is a difference of opinion, you should rely on the technical interpretation.

Technical analysis catches shifts before the fundamentalist can get adequate information. Changes within corporations often are taken into account by major investors long before they are announced or become public knowledge. When any stock moves two or three points in one day, the next morning's news will probably report that "Company officials know of no reason for the advance (or decline) in price."

28

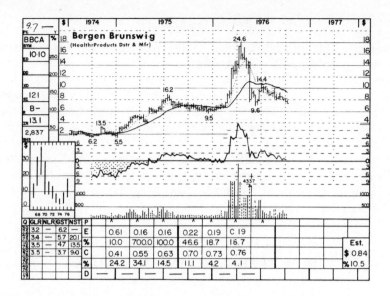

The proof will come weeks, even months, later, when the president will announce much higher (or lower) earnings, plans to enter a new, profitable market or unexpected losses due to production difficulties. The value of technical analysis is its ability to reflect what informed, and usually large, investors *think* or, more probably, *know*, will happen in the future.

The explanation: company officials are bound, by SEC regulations and by their ties as conscientious managers, to withhold good news and not to guess the future. But someone, through inside information or in-depth research, finds out what's really happening and starts to buy (or sell) heavily.

If you are interested in a certain stock whose price advances sharply in a short period, *buy*. If you wait for the announcement of the good news, you will miss your opportunity. Later, when you have the profits in hand, you can worry about the fundamental reasons why this action occurred. The same goes for selling.

HOW TECHNICAL ANALYSIS FORECASTS THE FUTURE

Time and again, the first indication of future news is signaled by technical analysis, specifically the chart of a stock. A good example was Bergen Brunswig (BBC), a company involved in the distribution of products and data processing for the health care field. I don't usually trade stocks listed on the American Stock Exchange (AMEX) but, in this case, did so because of the personal involvement of several of my clients.

In late 1975, the stock jumped from just over 7 to 17⅞ with ever-increasing volume. This was a handsome paper profit but I did not sell because there were prospects of higher earnings.

When the stock dropped back to 16, I assumed that this was a normal correction. But the decline continued. The stock broke through the uptrend line, so I sold quickly. This was a sign that some major investors were not only taking profits but were moving out of the stock. The chart said they suspected trouble ahead.

In the next few weeks, BBC fell to 8. Then came the bad news: Bergen Brunswig was losing a bundle on its contract to handle health care data processing for the state of North Carolina. Now do you wonder why I pay heed to technical analysis?

HOW TECHNICAL ANALYSIS WORKS

Customers often ask me, "Is technical analysis alone, without reference to other factors which affect the value of a stock, valid in forecasting the direction of future price changes?" My answer: "A qualified Yes."

The basis of technical analysis is the study of supply-and-demand conditions affecting a market or a stock. It is a simple method of arriving at buy and sell decisions. Most investors probably use it without even knowing they do so. This occurs when they say, "Looks good on the tape" or "I'm doubtful about the quality." You may not admit it, but such judgments involve the supply-and-demand factors relating to a stock.

A technician makes a conscious effort to use the past price movements to forecast future activity. He records, for later study, the significant transactions in a particular stock. He believes that what has happened before will be repeated, and so current movement can be used for future projections.

In large investment organizations, technical data are fed into a computer so that analyses and comparisons can be made electronically. But in most cases the information is plotted on charts. Hence, technicians often are known as chartists. The next chapter will explain how you can use charts effectively to achieve profits and to cut losses. Here's why:

Whenever a stock is traded on the NYSE, for fundamental, psychological or any other reasons, the transaction shows up on the chart. A steady inflow of capital must eventually force up the stock's price. And vice versa: a steady outflow of dollars from a stock must push down its price. It makes no difference whether this action is caused by insiders, institutions or the public. In the stock market, everybody's money is the same color. What *is* important is that accumulation (buying) usually creates a favorable chart pattern and distribution (selling) an unfavorable configuration.

TECHNICAL ANALYSIS IS NOT NEW

One of the reasons why many people avoid using technical analysis is the Wall Street–fostered idea that anything old or simple won't work in today's economy. The financial community has found that complicated concepts work well in selling securities to the public. The "experts," whether analysts, advisers or salesmen/brokers have discovered that when investors think that something is "new" or "ultracomplicated," it will work. This is not true.

I believe that nothing is new in the world of money. History is a cycle and repeats itself. Emphasis and interpretations change but the laws of supply and demand always work. Proper technical analysis is the way these powerful forces can be identified and used for stock market profits. It is especially valuable in determining whether and when to sell: *the most important decision any investor can make.* Of course, technical analysis is also valuable in buying.

The stock market is a numbers game, a statistics game. That's why charts can be useful. If you can be right on the sell side, you will be ahead of just about everybody else who is trading stocks and you will become a consistent winner. That's the basis of Blackman Strategy.

WHY I BECAME A TECHNICIAN

This conviction of the value of technical analysis dates back to 1966 when I was a thirty-year-old broker with Shearson Hammill. I had five years' experience and an income of about $18,000. Shearson Hammill, then one of the ten largest brokerage houses, called itself "The firm that research built." For years, its main advertising was a picture of a group of 30 or 40 people, its text boasting that "We spend $1 million a year to analyze securities."

That fall, it seemed to me that we were going into a bull market. The question in my mind was What stocks to buy?

I believed then, as I do now, that, in order to make substantial capital gains, it is necessary to concentrate capital. I decided to put approximately 25 percent of my clients' money into Beckman Instruments (BEC). The basis of my recommendation was both fundamental and technical. At that time, medical electronics was an emerging field. I felt it had good potential. The industry, which was a side benefit of the space exploration program, was in its infancy. There were virtually no hospitals with ICUs (Intensive Care Units), screening devices and other sophisticated health aids. Technically, BEC appeared to be ready to become a powerful UP stock.

I worked hard to get clients interested in purchasing Beckman, and finally

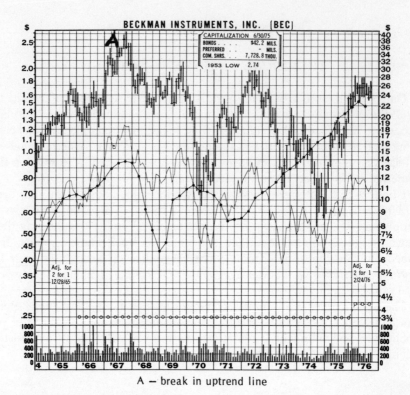

BECKMAN INSTRUMENTS, INC. (BEC)

CAPITALIZATION 6/30/75
BONDS . . . . $42.2 MILS.
PREFERRED . . - MILS.
COM. SHRS. . . 7,728.8 THOU.

1953 LOW 2.74

Adj. for
2 for 1
12/28/65

Adj. for
2 for 1
2/24/76

A — break in uptrend line

succeeded in accumulating a position of almost 7,500 shares at price levels between 35 and 45. As the stock moved higher, I kept buying "up," using the added value for more margin. I had all of my personal market money in 400 shares. The fundamentals looked sensational; the chart was good; the stock continued to rise.

Twelve months later, when the stock was near 80, I was still buying. I was confident that BEC could break 100.

Over one weekend, technical analysis changed my opinion. When looking at the BEC chart, I saw that the UP channel had been violated. Technically, the stock had topped out. (See Point A on the chart, with an adjustment for a 2-for-1 stock split in 1976.) BEC was no longer an UP stock; at worst, it was due for a drop; at best, it would go through a period of consolidation with no profits to traders.

This was a long, tough weekend for this thirty-year-old broker. I had more than $600,000 of my clients' money invested in this one stock. The chart had given a clearcut signal to sell.

On Monday morning, I couldn't wait to speak to the head electronics analyst. I explained that, although Beckman was not on Shearson's Buy List, it was a major NYSE-listed company and I had been buying heavily for over a year. I asked his opinion on whether or not to sell.

The analyst did not hesitate to tell me, "The stock looks good. The fundamentals are sound and I see no reason to liquidate."

I was not convinced. I pointed out that the BEC chart had broken through the uptrend line and was no longer in an UP drive. As a technician, I was concerned.

The analyst took the company line by saying, "Shearson Hammill is a fundamental firm and does not believe in charts." In essence, he told me that no analyst was allowed to be a technician. Yet I knew that some of the best-producing brokers kept charts in the bottom drawers of their desks.

He repeated that he was not a chartist and ended the interview with the comment, "Charts really don't mean a damn thing anyway."

I was not satisfied, so I checked with Shearson's broker on the floor of the stock exchange. His answer was identical. "The stock is acting fine. Do not worry. It's still a winner."

The moment of truth had arrived. Many of my smaller accounts had all of their money in Beckman. So did I.

That night I decided to recommend the complete liquidation of Beckman—to put my money (and my clients') where the chart was.

The next morning I told my customers that I was now a 100 percent technician and that, although my Research Department disagreed, I was convinced that the stock was now a sale. I suggested they sell every share as quickly as possible.

Luckily the majority of my clients listened. Within one year, BEC dropped from 80 to 42. Because of reliance on technical analysis, we sold the stock precisely at the high. The next year it did rally to 60, but the following year, it went down to 20.

This experience proved to be a pivotal decision for me. It made me a chartist forever. I became a brokers' broker and was sought out by many colleagues who asked advice on the art of selling.

THE IMPORTANCE OF SELLING RIGHT

In the brokerage business, a registered representative (RR) has three ways by which to build a clientele to the magic $100,000 a year gross commission level. He can:

1. Keep soliciting new accounts. That's hard, slow work that requires more patience than I have

2. Make money for his clients directly or by working with them so that his commissions will increase with the growth of their invested capital

3. Use a combination of both

For me, #3 has been most effective. When BEC "hit," it provided a financial base for me and for many of my clients. I was able to give my family a larger home and use part of the new capital to form Black Stein Kimball, Inc. My clientele recognized me as a broker who blended the fundamental with the purely technical approach. And, most important, I learned that only through this combination can the elusive talent of timing be attained and made to work profitably.

This principle, and my confidence in technical analysis, was proven again about a month after the Beckman success. This time I was trading the stock of a large electronics company on the Shearson Recommended List. The chart was not favorable.

Over the research wire (a separate communications system that large brokerage firms use to provide reams of research to their RRs to "keep them informed and up-to-date") came an estimate that third-quarter earnings of this company would be up 25 percent. The prediction was signed by the same analyst who had been so wrong on Beckman. This forecast, incidentally, was made two weeks after the quarter had officially ended—time enough for corporate management to have a pretty good idea of results.

A few days later, the official company report came out: Earnings were *down* from those of the previous year! The stock was clobbered. Three of my clients, with a total of 2,200 shares of this "great" stock, did not heed my technical-based warning. They all lost money. One client left me and the others were angry and upset.

What had happened, of course, was that the naïve analyst had accepted the company's optimistic evaluation and, without digging further or checking the stock's market action, had passed the exaggerated data on to RRs and their clients. One required trait for every security analyst, especially those who do not pay attention to charts, is a healthy dose of skepticism. Our man did not have it.

This episode reinforced my belief in technical analysis. I vowed that, to protect my clients, I would never again recommend the purchase or sale of any stocks without making a complete technical study. *My rule: If the issue is weak technically, always avoid purchase.*

IMPORTANCE OF CHARTS

The methods used in analyzing the stock market are quite different today from those used in the mid-1960s. All major institutions have at least one technician on their staff, and my guess is that the majority of portfolio managers are straight technicians.

One of my friends runs a $700 million growth mutual fund with the same two graphic tools I rely on: a long-term chart book and a daily chart service.

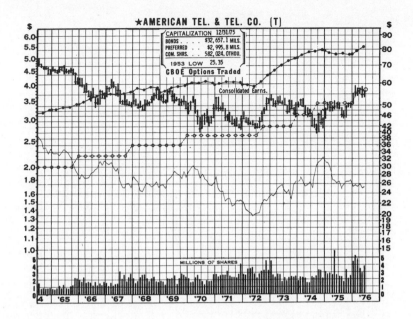

CAPITALIZATION 12/31/75
BONDS . . . . $32,657.1 MILS.
PREFERRED . . $2,995.8 MILS.
COM. SHRS. . . 582,024. OTHOU.
1953 LOW 25.35
CBOE Options Traded
Consolidated Earns.
MILLIONS OF SHARES

Their total cost is $359 plus first-class postage. That's a tiny sum for such a huge portfolio. Yet virtually all his decisions are based on review and interpretation of those charts!

This reliance on technical analysis may seem surprising, but it's true. Even if you are skeptical about charting as an aid in trading and investing, you should know what and how these professional money men think.

As you will learn by experience, charts are descriptive. They portray the distinct character of each stock. The chart of AT&T, for example, moves within a relatively narrow range with small, slow fluctuations. This reflects its shareholders: trust funds and older people seeking security and income.

The chart of Fairchild Camera & Instrument Corp. (FCI) is volatile, with wide price swings: rapid rises in boom times and fast, steep declines when corporate profits sag. Obviously, FCI is a favorite of speculators who trade for a few points.

IMPORTANCE OF PSYCHOLOGY

Keep in mind that a great deal of investing is psychological. That's another advantage of technical analysis. It reports what's happening. When the trend is up, people buy more and are willing to pay ever higher prices. When the trend is down, they stop buying and, in most cases, start to sell.

Here again, technical analysis calls the shots. It is a tool you cannot afford to neglect. It is the base for almost all successful trading in the stock market.

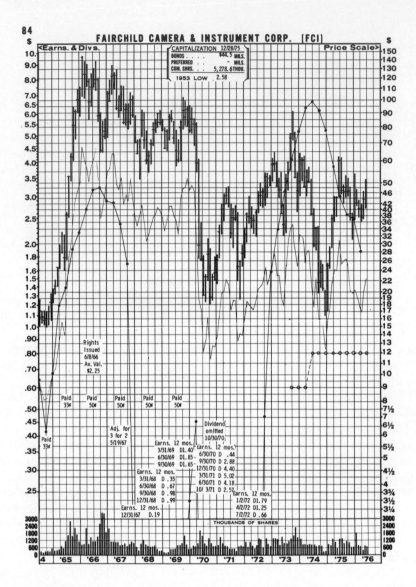

Charts do not work *all* the time but they do work *most* of the time. They give you the overall direction of a market and/or of a stock. In making your buy and sell decisions, use a blend of fundamental and technical analysis. But if the fundamentals look good and the charts look bad, let the technical picture be the deciding factor. Your profits will be greater and your losses fewer.

Now let's look at one of the most valuable technical indicators: the London Stock Market Index.

5. Watch the London Stock Market Index

Many times in the past few years when I was uncertain about the trend of the stock market, I have said, "God Bless England." The reason is the London Financial Times Index. This is somewhat like a Dow Jones Industrial Average for the London Stock Exchange. Each weekday morning the Dow Jones news ticker reports the previous day's close, the latest average and the last prices of such well-known international corporations as Beecham, British-American Tobacco and Imperial Chemical Industries. (Remember, the British market opens three hours ahead of New York.)

Over the years I have found the British Industrial Average to be one of the most accurate technical forecasters of the U.S. stock market. As you can see from the chart on pages 40 and 41, London stock prices are closely related to the NYSE. What happens in Britain will take place in the United States generally one cycle later. Sometimes the action will be as close as the same day; usually it will occur within a week; occasionally there will be a delay of two weeks or more. But at all times there is a strong relationship because present-day financial markets are worldwide.

In my experience, the greatest use of the London market is in timing. When the British action is positive (a breakthrough on the upside), this is almost always a buy signal. When the Index is negative, I become cautious and consider selling because I know this will have a dampening effect on the prices of U.S. securities and usually will indicate future trouble. By plotting trendlines, you can catch major shifts in investor sentiment and be in a position to act before the trend is apparent in America.

HOW LONDON FORECASTS NEW YORK

Check the Multi-Average to see how frequently the London market forecasts American activity:

In December 1956, London bottomed at 170 while the Dow fell to 455 two weeks later.

In April 1957, London peaked at 210. Within weeks, the Dow started up, hitting a high of 520 about two months later, in June.

In January 1958, London was down to 154. This time, the U.S. reaction was earlier as the Dow fell back to 416. Then came a long rally: in the U.S. the peak came earlier: a high of 688 in December 1959. London's rise, to a high of 340, did not come until February.

In 1961, the traditional pattern was again reversed: the Dow high, 741, came in December, some five months ahead of the London high of 365. But then the parallel started again: London dropped to 252 in the spring of 1962 with the Dow following closely, bottoming at 524 about the same time.

In 1966, London fell to 284 in October. The Dow, after breaking the 1,000 mark, followed by a dip to 735.

In 1968, London soared to 521 in October, presaging the Dow's December rise to 994.

In 1970, London dropped to 315 in April, signaling the Dow's decline to 627 in May. Then came the big rally, with London reaching a new high of 543 in July. This time, the U.S. was slower to react and did not reach its new high for another six months.

In 1974, London fell to 144 in the late fall. This forecast the U.S. drop to 570 in December.

In 1975–76, the relationship continued: London moved from a low of 146 to 418 in January. The Dow followed to a high of 1,018 in March. In the late spring, when the Dow was about 850, London rallied to 420, then ran out of steam and dropped back again. In the U.S., the Dow tried to break through for five months and, after a midsummer rally, fell back pretty much in line with the London activity.

I'll grant that the relationship is not always the same, but 90 percent of the time what happens abroad will be reflected here. Sometimes—in fact, often—it's hard to accept the predictions, but, with experience, you will pay more and more attention to this international barometer.

The effectiveness of this technical indicator is logical. There are close parallels in the British and American socioeconomic patterns: the United States has shifted from a consuming to a producing nation and is deeply involved in international business; and today, all financial markets involve every major nation. Top professional money managers around the world take the global view. Fortunately, those of us who do not have the research facilities to follow international finance can rely on the London Index.

USING CHARTS

The easiest way to get maximum benefit from the action of the London Exchange is by a chart with channels and uptrend lines. When they break, up or down, act immediately. In the majority of situations you will boost your gains and cut your losses.

To keep abreast, you can buy a wall chart to show quarterly activity of the major stock market averages (Dow Jones Industrials, S&P Industrials, British Industrials) and business indexes (Federal Reserve Board Production Index, Gross National Product, Earnings per Share), etc. This wall chart costs $12 from United Business Service, 210 Newbury Street, Boston, Mass. 02116.

If you prefer to keep more current and can spend 15 minutes a week, make your own guide by drawing in lines showing the weekly closing prices of the London Index. Or ask your RR to duplicate the London chart so you can use it with your long-term records.

CHECK YOUR BROKER'S KNOWLEDGE

Most Wall Streeters are not familiar with the London Exchange. Many RRs think of England only as a place where gold is traded or where Sherlock Holmes solved murder mysteries. Next time you choose a broker, add this question to your others: "How much do you know about the London Index?"

This knowledge can be important in trading. When the broker gets to work, he can check the news ticker to get the early morning action of the London market, which has already been active for three hours. By lunchtime in New York, London will be closed. That means you still have plenty of time to use the final prices to help make your investment decisions.

More complete details are available on the financial pages of major daily newspapers. Check the closing price of the London market each week against the chart and watch the trend—as is explained in the next chapter.

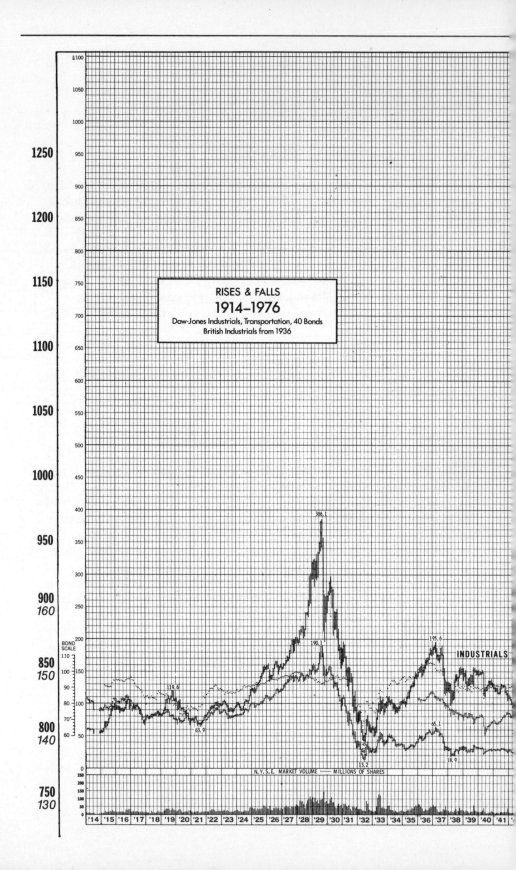

RISES & FALLS
1914–1976
Dow-Jones Industrials, Transportation, 40 Bonds
British Industrials from 1936

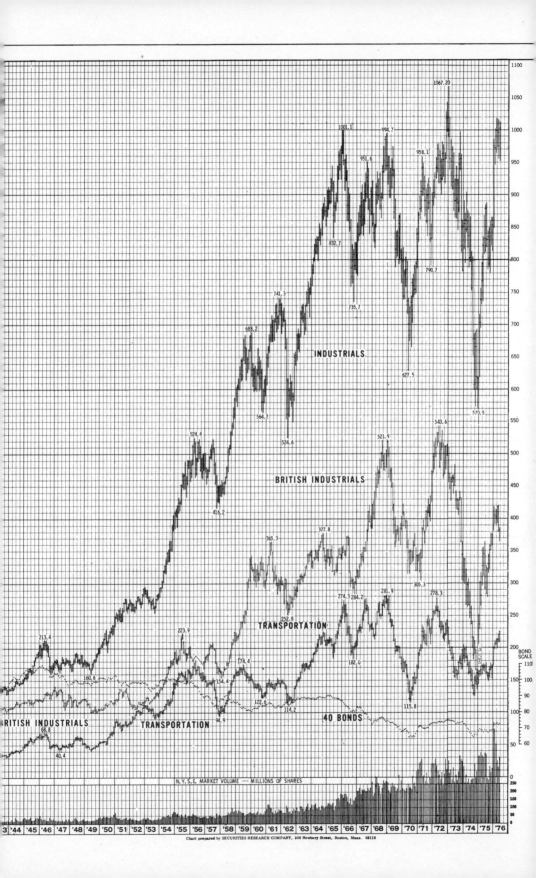

1100
1050
1067.20
1001.1
994.7
1000
951.6
958.1
950
900
832.7
790.7
850
800
INDUSTRIALS
741.3
735.7
750
688.2
700
627.5
650
570.0
600
564.2
550
524.4
524.6
521.9
543.6
500
BRITISH INDUSTRIALS
450
416.2
400
377.8
365.3
350
305.3
278.3
300
274.3 284.2
281.9
252.8
250
223.9
213.4
182.0
TRANSPORTATION
200
174.4
BOND
SCALE
160.6
110
154.4
150
100
122.6
90
115.8
114.2
BRITISH INDUSTRIALS
94.9
40 BONDS
80
TRANSPORTATION
100
68.8
70
40.4
60

N. Y. S. E. MARKET VOLUME — MILLIONS OF SHARES
250
200
150
100
50

3 '44 '45 '46 '47 '48 '49 '50 '51 '52 '53 '54 '55 '56 '57 '58 '59 '60 '61 '62 '63 '64 '65 '66 '67 '68 '69 '70 '71 '72 '73 '74 '75 '76

Chart prepared by SECURITIES RESEARCH COMPANY, 208 Newbury Street, Boston, Mass. 02116

6.   How to Plot and Read a Chart

Preparing a chart is easy; reading and interpreting it is more difficult. But it's not that complicated. Anyone who has been smart enough to accumulate money can learn to use charts profitably. It takes a couple of hours a week to build, maintain and "read" the few charts needed to cover the stocks owned or being considered for purchase.

With all charts, look for trends: UP trends for stocks to buy; DOWN trends for stocks to avoid or sell. For financial success you must watch charts over a period of time. In a few weeks or months, you will discover developing patterns, which can be compared with charts of the previous performance of this stock, its group and the general market.

The two most commonly used types of charts are Point & Figure (P&F) and Bar. For best results, both should be constructed on a daily or weekly basis. If you are a do-it-yourselfer, all you need is the daily or weekly stock market reports and a pad of graph paper: plain squares for P&F charts; logarithmic or grid paper for Bar charts.

For most people, however, it's more convenient to buy printed charts as outlined in this chapter.

Many technicians rely on P&F charts but, for my part, I have not found them effective or easy to interpret. They are one-dimensional graphics that show price changes only in relation to previous price changes. There are no indications of time or volume.

BAR CHARTS

I believe in Bar charts. Here the horizontal axis represents time; the vertical coordinates refer to price. Volume is shown by vertical lines at the

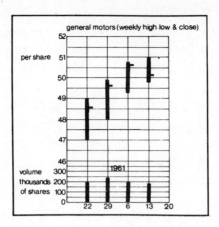

bottom. (For details, see the explanation of the Legend chart, a Bar chart.)

To build a Bar chart, enter a dot representing the highest price at which the stock traded, then another dot for the low. Connect the dots and add a horizontal nub to make the closing price. From the bottom up, draw a vertical line to record the volume. Each vertical line depicts the activity for the selected time period: one day, a week or a month.

In the illustration, the high price for General Motors on the first week was 49, the low 47, and the close 48¼. On week 2, the high was 49⅞, the low 48, and the close 49¼. The weekly volumes were 200,000 shares and about 225,000 shares respectively. The figures 22, 29, etc. show the date of the week.

Notice how, after a number of entries, the lines begin to form a meaning-ful pattern, in this case, a definite UPtrend.

EXPLANATION OF LEGEND CHART

This logarithmic chart, available from Securities Research Company (see Glossary under Chart Services), is typical of the information provided by printed chart services. Here's how to use it:

Left-hand side: 0 to 5.50 is the base for (a) earnings for the past 22 months as shown by the solid line which most of the time runs above the price notations; (b) dividends at the annual rate, as detailed in the split line near the bottom of the chart. The X indicates the week of ex-dividend: the 0, the week the dividend payment was made.

Right-hand side: The dollar value per share of the stock—in this illustra-tion, 0 to 82. These numbers are also used with the Ratio-Cator.

This price range is equal to 15 times the earnings-and-dividend scale at the left. Thus, when the price bars and the earnings lines coincide, the price is 15 times earnings—as in early June 1976.

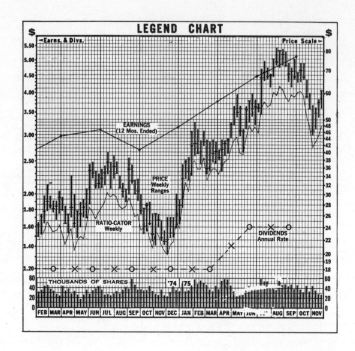

Vertical and crossbars: Vertical bars depict the range of the week's highest and lowest prices with the crossbar noting the last trading price for the week.

In February 1974, this stock traded between 22½ and 32, then moved down to 23, up to a high of 34 in April, down to a low of 22¼ in May, etc. The lowest quotation was 20, in December 1974; the highest, about 83 in August 1975; the last sale was at 61, in November 1976.

Ratio-Cator Line: This is typical of the special computations developed by chart services as sales tools. This is a reference point. It indicates whether the stock has kept pace, outperformed or lagged behind the general market as indicated by the Dow Average.

These data are obtained by dividing the closing price of the stock by the closing price of the Dow on the same day. The resulting percentage is multiplied by a factor of 7.0 to bring the line closer to the price bars. Read this checkpoint from the right-hand scale.

Bottom: The months and years are spelled out. The volume traded each week is shown by the vertical bars. These are plotted on an arithmetical scale in thousands of shares.

This chart utilizes a ratio scale: i.e., the price range, earnings and dividend information are plotted on uniform-rate-scale (semilogarithmic) grids. The vertical line distance for a 100 percent move is the same any place on the chart, irrespective of whether the rise is from $5 to $10 or from $30 to $60. This permits direct comparison with any other chart.

Other charts are basically the same. Each service has its own style but the important trend information is clearly shown by the chart formation.

THE IMPORTANCE OF TRENDLINES

Technicians use scores of chart patterns but the easiest to construct, to understand and to use profitably are trendlines. These are formed by using a ruler to draw a straight line connecting the last two or three low prices *at the bottom*. This forms an UPtrendline which, under Blackman Strategy, is the key to successful trading. This is the support level and provides the frame of reference for buying.

As the price movement changes, draw new lines to keep the chart current. It is not necessary to draw in the top trendline at the outset. This is a sell line and can be developed after you have purchased the stock.

The importance of the UPtrendline is that it *always* points to possible gains in the stock. The closer to the trendline you buy, the greater your trading profits. But with a real winner, you can buy above the trendline and still do well.

In my experience, trendlines are the best of all chart patterns. They work for me, and my clients consistently make money. They are easy to spot and to follow and their signals are clear. Disregard all other chart formations and techniques. I believe that their interpretations are as beneficial as the knowledge gained by people in the Middle Ages when sages argued about how many angels were on the head of a pin. Useless information seldom makes—and usually loses—money.

With Blackman Strategy, look for charts only of stocks in an UPtrend: when the trendlines are slanting UP.

DOWNtrendlines, of course, are the opposite. They are formed by connecting the last two or three tops. Since they form a DOWN pattern, skip the chart and move to another stock.

WHAT TO DO WITH AN UPTRENDING STOCK

Once you find a chart with a favorable pattern, be patient. The trends do not always work out, and when they do, they may take time—usually weeks, often months. This gives you a chance to do your homework:

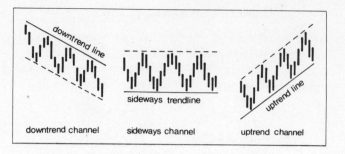

downtrend channel   sideways channel   uptrend channel

1. Check the group
2. Review the intermediate and long-term charts for perspective
3. Watch the over-all stock market

Let's use Howard Johnson (HJ) as an example of a stock that *may* be worth buying. In November 1976, the HJ chart showed an UPtrend: from 9½ in early October to about 10¾.

To find out if this might be an isolated move, check the industry group: in the front pages of the chart books, in the weekly listings in *Barron's* and in the Associated Press summaries.

Note: If one stock moves up while the rest of its group is neutral or trending down, watch out. Whatever is happening involves only that one corporation. It may be a merger, acquisition, new product, etc. Do not buy such a stock except as a sheer speculation.

HoJo was a representative of two industry groups: hotel-motels and restaurants. Both were promising, and a further check showed that the leaders were stirring: Hilton Hotels had just broken into a new high; Holiday Inns was rising, and Ramada Inns had reversed a long downtrend, and in the past week had been one of the Ten Most Active stocks on the NYSE. The group might not yet be in a real uptrend but the downtrend had been reversed.

Now that you may have a winner, review HJ's action over the past two years on the top chart on page 47. To understand the swings and get a feel of how the stock acts, draw channels of previous movements by connecting the bottoms for the basic trendline and by joining the tops to form a parallel line within which the price shifts occurred.

Note that the swings have been within fairly narrow ranges, about 50% of the basic value: from a low of 10½ to a high of 15; from about 13¾ to just over 17. This indicates that the most recent channel is in character.

Finally study the long-term action on the 12-year chart (bottom of page 47). This shows that, historically, HJ has been more volatile than indicated by the two-year chart. There have been wide, long swings up and down. Again, draw channels to get an idea of the relative movement. Except for

HOWARD JOHNSON CO. (HJ)

Restaurants and motor hotels in many states (mostly in the East) and abroad.

P-B-W Options Traded

Pd. 5¢	Pd. 6¢	Pd. 6¢	Pd. 6¢	Pd. 6¢	Pd. 7¢	Pd. 7¢
4/30/75	7/31/75	10/31/75	1/30/76	4/30/76	7/30/76	10/29/76

'75 '76   '76

MAR APR MAY JUN JUL AUG SEP OCT NOV DEC JAN FEB MAR APR MAY JUN JUL AUG SEP OCT NOV DEC

HOWARD JOHNSON CO. (HJ)

CAPITALIZATION	1/2/76	
BONDS	$3.7	MILS.
PREFERRED . .	-	MILS.
COM. SHRS. . .	21,925.0	THOU.

1953 LOW -

P-B-W Options Traded

	Adj. for 2% S/D 3/14/66	Paid 2.5¢	Paid 10¢	Paid 11¢	Paid 12¢	Paid 12¢	Paid 13¢	Paid 18¢	Paid 20¢	Also pd. 10¢
Adj. for 2% S/D 5/3/65	Adj. for 2 for 1 5/20/66	Adj. for 1% S/D 5/10/67		Adj. for 2 for 1 5/20/69			Adj. for 2 for 1 8/8/72			

4 '65 '66 '67 '68 '69 '70 '71 '72 '73 '74 '75 '76

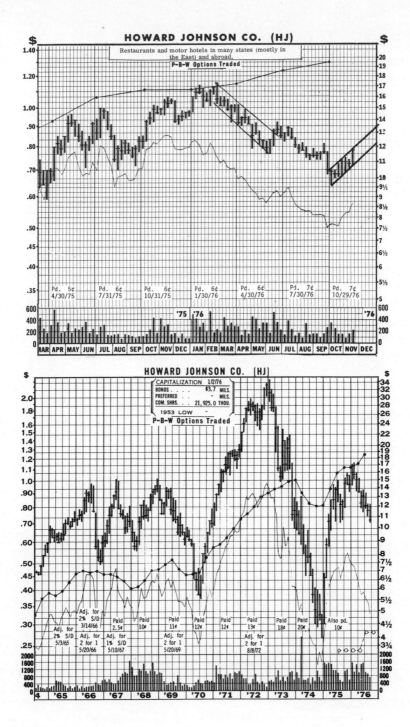

the 1975–76 broad channel, the stock has held within a narrow range. This is further confirmation that the latest action is accurate.

At all times, check the volume—at the bottom of the chart. Clearly the recent activity has been modest. Watch for higher sales to make the beginning of a profitable UPtrend.

With HJ, both the stock and the groups look OK, so now you have to wait for the market to swing up. This gives you an opportunity to project possible profits: 20 percent for industrial/service corporations; 10 percent for utilities.

HOW TO MAKE PROJECTIONS

Normally, the top line of a channel will parallel the UPtrendline. Remember, to be a valid channel, the top line *must* be parallel to the UPtrendline. You do not have to have a channel to trade profitably but it's a convenient guide. It shows the probable range of price fluctuations. Usually, a channel takes time to develop, but in some cases, such as Litton Industries (page 63) and Pittston Co. (page 52) where the stocks shoot almost straight up, the channel develops later, after the spike up.

When you draw the channels, make the bottom UPtrendline as tight as possible. This is your *buy* point. The top of the channel marks the *sell* point. Trading takes place within the channel. Cyclical stocks will move in that area for three to six months. Most stocks tend to have similar patterns and thus similar channel widths. The trader will buy at the bottom and sell at the top. Buy again when there's a dip—as long as the overall trend is UP.

Trading can be a continuous process and does not require a purchase

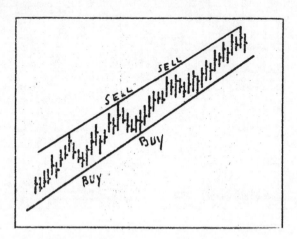

exactly at the bottom. If the stock is still in its channel after five or six months, it's still OK to buy if there appears to be a potential for that 20 percent gain.

The channel is useful for projections. This can be done by extending the channel as far as possible: with HJ, to a high of about 13½ and a low of 12. These should be updated as the stock moves ahead.

Note: If the tops are so erratic that you cannot project the channel, draw a line connecting the bottoms and then pencil in a parallel top line at a distance similar to the historical width pattern.

With HJ, you are now in a position to act. It looks like an UP stock in an UP group. If the market is strong, and you are optimistic, you may want to bargain-hunt by buying at about 12. This decision depends on whether and for how long you are willing to tie up your money while waiting. Often a stock will move to the top of its channel, then turn down to a higher-than-before bottom.

Keep in mind that when you trade by charts, you will never buy at the bottom or sell at the top. You will strive to catch the bulk of the price rise and take your 20 percent profit.

WHAT COULD HAPPEN

Let's suppose that a month later, a newly drawn channel indicates that HJ can go to 17. The stock is still moving within its channel, so you have working room: you can try to buy at 12 and sell at 15 to make your target profit or buy at 13 and sell at 16.

In a strong market. I would buy at 12, set a mental stop at 15, and let my profits run. My gain will be greater than if I had been conservative, but so will the risk. As a policy, I prefer to sell too soon. I know that with a 20 percent gain four times a year, I can double my capital every 12 months.

The charts show why 17 is a key point. It's a resistance level—where the stock reached an interim high early in 1976 and the price from which the steep drop started in late 1973.

In both cases, the people who bought at 17 and still hold the stock will unload to break even. It's also the point at which chart readers who bought in around 12 will start to take their profits.

Do not be greedy. After a strong upmove, stocks begin to consolidate and then back down to get ready for the next push. By selling at the top of the channel, I can take my gains and reinvest at the lower, pull-back price.

I sell at the top of the channel 95 percent of the time. I follow the leaders. The only exceptions are when: (1) the market is ultrastrong—then I might try for a few extra points, but I will use mental stops to protect my gain; (2)

the stock is near or through an interim or all-time high. This could be the Big Move every trader hopes for.

Note: HJ was a good example of a hope that failed. The uptrend did not continue. Always wait for confirmation before you buy!

WHAT TO DO WITH A downTRENDING STOCK

When there's a clear downtrend in the chart of the overall market, go into cash. When a stock heads down, get out fast. In both cases, there's no way to know how far the drop will go.

If it's a quality stock, keep an eye on its chart, and when you see that there's a consolidation period where the downtrend seems to be halting and the movement is within a narrow range, keep watch. This may be the start of a reversal, a very important signal. Wait for the uptrend to start, and when it's confirmed, start buying when both the group and market action are favorable.

McDonald's is an excellent illustration of how to take advantage of a reversal. In late 1974, as the result of the oil crisis, this quality stock lost nearly two thirds of its value as it went to the low 20s. There was a short period of sideways movement to form a bottom base. There was another short dip, but then came the start of the uptrend. When this continued, it was a signal to buy.

downtrends are important only when they reverse and start up again.

BREAKOUTS FOR BIG GAINS

Charts are about the only way a small investor can spot a breakout. An upside breakout usually signals a change in the equilibrium in the supply-demand equation affecting an issue. It should be identified and acted upon just as soon as it occurs. There are two types of real breakouts. They are both into new highs: interim and all-time.

Interim. This is a high above the top of the past two or three years. The longer the time between the interim highs, the greater the chance of a strong upmove when and if there is a breakthrough. When this surge occurs in less than one year, you can get bagged by sellers who are looking for quick profits and/or by people who bought at the old high and want to get out even.

All-time. This means a record price for the stock. When this happens, the stock will act like a high flyer or shooting star. Its movement will accelerate like O. J. Simpson after he has made it through the line. Forget about everything else and let your profits run. As long as the upmove continues, you have nothing to worry about. This could be a Big Hit with a 50 percent or more gain in six months or less.

Be patient. True upside breakouts do not occur often. The most powerful are based on a V formation.

We can see what happened with Pittston Co. (PCO) in early 1975. At 22, the stock broke into an all-time high, above the peak of early 1971.

The chart called the shots: a strong UPtrend. At the same time, the fundamentals were good: (1) Full year earnings were not available but were likely to be over $3.00 a share, far above the 70¢ of the year before; (2) The

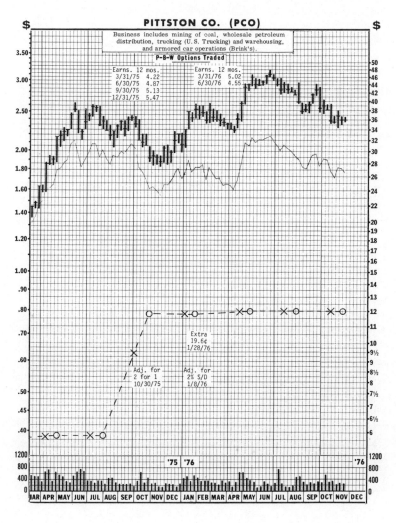

PITTSTON CO. (PCO)

Business includes mining of coal, wholesale petroleum distribution, trucking (U.S. Trucking) and warehousing, and armored car operations (Brink's).

P-B-W Options Traded

Earns. 12 mos.		Earns. 12 mos.	
3/31/75	4.22	3/31/76	5.02
6/30/75	4.87	6/30/76	4.55
9/30/75	5.13		
12/31/75	5.47		

Extra
19.6¢
1/28/76

Adj. for
2 for 1
10/30/75

Adj. for
2% S/D
1/8/76

price of coal was in the process of quadrupling; (3) PCO was a big, quality, A-rated company. Its sales were over $1 billion, and, with 36 million shares, it was attractive to institutional investors.

The technical outlook was just as great: (1) The chart signaled that something big was happening; (2) The volume indicated that the Big Boys were buying; (3) The V formation was significant; and (4) The overall market was strong.

By long-term standards, the stock was undervalued: selling at a price/ earnings ratio of 7, which was at the low end of its historical range of 14–7.6. The stage was set for a profit-making double play: higher earnings

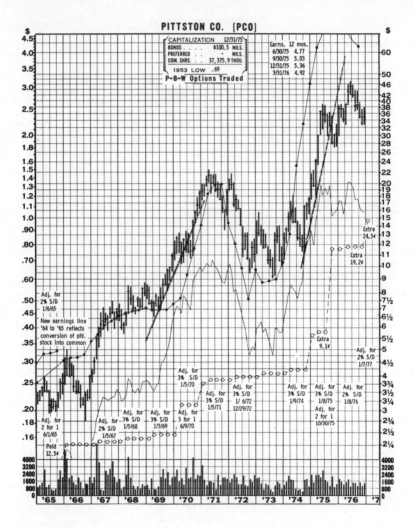

and a higher multiple. At 10 times $3.00 per share profits, the stock would sell at 30. With greater investor enthusiasm, it could go much higher.

PCO performed as the chart predicted. From the breakout at 22, it moved almost straight up to 40, where it broke down through the trendline to signal Sell. Sure, it did sputter up to 48, but the chartist would have taken his gains at about 36 when the dip started. This was a 64 percent gain in less than six months.

WHY BREAKOUTS WORK

Breakouts into new highs work because there are no sellers left. Everyone has a profit and no one is interested in selling. When the Big Boys move in, as shown by the higher volume, they have to pay more and more. The stampede is on and will continue as long as the overall market stays strong.

Should you sell into a breakout? Sometimes. It depends on the stock, the group, the market and your purchase price. Not all breakouts pan out as is explained later with Bucyrus-Erie. Yet, when the breakout is genuine, the profits can be big and quick.

Generally speaking, if you have a 20 percent profit, sell into the strength of this updrive *unless* there is a very strong market and equally vigorous group activity. If the stock does continue to go up, you can always buy in on a pullback and still make a bundle. With PCO, if you bought at 17, a sale at 22 would be profitable. A buy-back at 24 would work well. And even at 32, you would make your 20 percent profit.

Advice: When a significant UP breakthrough takes place, check the Sell rules. If a single one flashes a signal, do not argue. Get out. If the overall market is buoyant and you still like the group, switch to another holding in the same industry. With hotel-motels: from HJ to Hilton or Holiday Inns, if one of these stocks is near the bottom of its UP trendline. With Hilton at 20 and still moving ahead, there's still a chance for that 20 percent gain with a rise to 24.

DOWNSIDE BREAKTHROUGHS

When a breakout is on the downside, through the UP trendline, sell or get ready to sell. Make sure that this is the real thing by waiting until the drop is a maximum of 3 percent. Otherwise you can be caught by intermittent fluctuations.

Get out fast, because there is no way to predict how far the stock may fall—in 1973–74, HJ dropped from 20 to 4! The point to sell was at 16½.

Always heed the chart. The downmove was clear, and even though there was a temporary upmove, the stock swung back and dived almost straight down to 5¾, then rallied, but finally bottomed at 4.

(*See Chapter 7 for more information.*)

GENERAL COUNSEL

Keep your charts up-to-date (or have your broker do it). At the end of each week, mark in the highs and lows, re-form your trendlines and extend the channels as far as the chart permits.

A chart is a frame of reference, not a set-in-concrete signaler. By learning to draw your own charts, or to keep current purchased ones, you can find stocks in an uptrend and avoid or sell those that are going down. This way you will make more money and also reduce your losses.

7. How to Use Charts to Boost Profits and Cut Losses

"Trading in the stock market is a battle," said Gerald Loeb, a true financial expert and author of two best-selling books, *The Battle for Investment Survival,* and *The Battle for Stock-Market Profits.* I agree. In investing in securities, you are competing with some of the smartest and toughest people in the world. I believe the way to win is to follow their lead and use their actions to your advantage. That's why charts are so important. *The proper use of charts is the core of Blackman Strategy.*

As explained earlier, charts are visual reports of what has happened and is happening in the overall stock market, in industry groups and in specific stocks. They show the shifts in investor interest—especially the psychological swings which are so important in successful trading.

Chartists do not worry about the "why." They act on the "what." They know that charts are accurate because they reflect supply and demand—the forces that establish trends and provide momentum for change. If you have ever been in battle or competitive sports, you know the importance of momentum. It is just as vital in the stock market. When there's momentum in the overall market or in any individual stock, the action will continue to accelerate. If it's on the upside, the trend will be higher and higher. If it's on the downside, the stock values will continue to fall.

USING CHARTS YOURSELF

Anyone can make their own charts but most people prefer to rely on printed reports. I use three sets, the same as those that can be found on the desk of almost every professional money manager:

Long-term: Cycli-graphs, which show the 12-year history of 1,105 leading stocks, major industry groups and key market averages; *Medium-term:*

Trendline Current Market Perspectives, which chart 972 listed corporations for four years; *Short-term:* Trendline Daily Basis Charts, which provide similar information on a weekly basis for the past six months. (For information, and costs, see Glossary under Chart Services.)

If you can't afford all the chart books, buy the long-term one and let your broker keep you up to date with copies of weekly charts of stocks you own or consider buying.

When you are dealing with $5,000 or less, consider doing your own individual charts and making your own decisions. With larger investments, let your broker do the work. Of course, you can always set up your own chart-checking system. It takes time and commitment, but it can be fun and will give you a better understanding of why the Blackman Strategy is successful.

In the beginning, move slowly; concentrate on one or two stocks from your list of five prospects. It will require about three minutes a week to review both the long- and short-term chart books.

Play the game on paper: write your interpretation of what the chart signals and, in theory, act accordingly. It won't take you long to become an "expert," or at least proficient.

If you are still skeptical, or you want to bet a better perspective, chart all of the stocks you have traded in the last two years. Watch to see what would have happened if you had paid attention to the breaks in the trendlines or channels when buying or selling. This is an easy way to profit from your right moves and learn from your mistakes.

Another important consideration: Is your broker a technician? If he is familiar with technical analysis, he can be very helpful in guiding your research and in aiding you to develop the essential "feel" for chart signals and discipline to act on what the chart indicates, regardless of how high your hopes or how great your despair.

Once you have confidence in your chart-reading ability, especially using signals to time your buying and selling, watch for meaningful configurations: tops, downside breakthroughs, etc. Pay attention: Buy when the move is UP, liquidate when it's DOWN—just as I did with Beckman Instruments.

Then be patient. If the market is in a downswing, there will be virtually no stocks that can buck the tide. Do not try to locate such rarities. It's time-consuming, risky and, for amateurs who have to pay commissions, expensive.

POINT & FIGURE CHARTS

As stated earlier, there are two main types of charts: Point & Figure (P&F) and Bar. In building a P&F chart, entries are made only when the

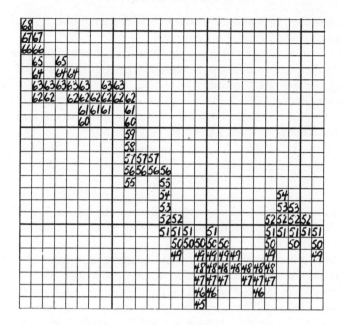

stock fluctuates a certain number of points: one, three or, occasionally, five. There are no considerations of volume and the passage of time.

This illustration (courtesy of Dun & Bradstreet's *Your Investments*) shows the trend of General Motors stock. The daily closing price is posted in a square, one above or below another, depending on the upward or downward movement. As long as the price continues in the same direction, the same column is used. When the price shifts direction, the figure is moved to the next column.

Here, GM fell in a downward sequence from 68 to 67 to 66. Then it rose to 67, so the chartist moved to column 2. After GM went down to 62 and up to 63, he shifted to column 3, etc.

P&F charts are simple, but I do not believe they are effective tools. To be honest, I think they are for illiterates who cannot or will not understand elementary addition and subtraction. *They do not work*. They are for people who want to believe they are charting, but who actually are merely going through the motions.

Here are some reasons why I do *not* use P&F charts:

• There is no room for volume—which is always worth noting, and on occasion can be significant;

• Only closing prices are recorded, so you may be faked out. During the day there can be wide swings between high and low;

• The structure of the chart prevents drawing trendlines to enable you to form all-important uptrends and channels;

• There is no frame of reference that can be used to determine when to buy or sell. All you are doing is plotting the price movements. This may be interesting, but it is not informative.

My advice: Avoid P&F charts. My guess is that in an UP market, you can do just as well in picking winners by throwing darts at the daily financial tables of the New York Stock Exchange.

BAR CHARTS

I am a Bar chartist. I am convinced that time and volume are important in reaching investment decisions on the market and are essential with individual stocks.

As explained earlier, Bar charts show changes in price and volume for specific periods of time: a day, a week, a month or longer. After a number of vertical lines (the price movement) have been entered on the chart, a pattern begins to form. This shows the trend: up, down or sideways.

These are the formations that are studied by chartists and used to project probable future stock, or market, action.

This is the time to draw those important trendlines: at first by using a straight edge to draw a line connecting the last two or three lows; later, if the direction is up, to draw the top trendline by connecting the most recent high points.

If the trendline is down or neutral, forget the stock and chart for the time being. Maintain and follow charts only of stocks that are beginning to show UPtrendlines. Otherwise you're wasting your time.

HOW CHARTS FLASH SIGNALS

Charts are the core of technical analysis. They show changes in supply and demand. These, in turn, reflect investor sentiment, which, realistically, is what the professional money managers feel, or often, know. Charts show changes that cannot be anticipated by fundamental analysis.

Repeat: If the trendline is not UP, sell, or do not buy. I believe this uptrend is the single most important signal of any chart. Find it early and you will gain maximum profits; follow it closely and you will learn the art of selling. And never argue with the chart.

Throughout this book are examples of how to use charts to profitable advantage—to time buying and selling.

Example: In 1962, the Dow Jones Industrial Average fell 27 percent between March and June—from 715 to 524. It was down 11 percent for the year. Yet there was no real slowdown in business for the next four years. The fundamentals may have appeared to be OK, but technical analysis, primarily charts, signaled problems ahead.

Somewhere over that year there was a change in investor sentiment. This may have been due to fundamental factors, but more likely it was psychological, as indicated by President Kennedy's reply to the question, Why are stocks going down? —"They are probably too high."

The charts caught the change and showed a reversal of the uptrend. By selling when there was a break in the uptrend line of the Dow (or of individual stocks), the astute investor avoided the debacle that followed.

Note: This was one lesson I learned the hard way. I refused to sell on the first breakthrough but managed to get out with losses averaging 15 percent—about half those of the overall market decline.

CHARTS DISCOUNT THE FUTURE

For emphasis, I'm repeating that a chart will also point out fundamental developments that are being discounted by major investors. This often occurs long before such changes are generally known. This change in investor sentiment appears as a break in the channel line.

Study the chart of Brunswick Corp. to see how clearly it predicted trouble: the 1969–70 drop, and especially the 1972 break that resulted in the horrendous decline from over 50 to 7.

In the same way, a chart breakthrough, on the upside, forecast the rise in 1970–71 and in 1974–75.

Note how proper interpretation made it possible to trade this stock profitably: almost all uptrends were good for a 20 percent (or more) gain, and the down signals were strong enough to let you get out quickly. It's always easier with hindsight!

MAKING MONEY WITH NEW HIGHS

If you've made money with a stock in the past, keep tabs on its progress. With Blackman Strategy, you may be able to do even better the second or third time you trade, even though its price has moved up sharply.

This was the situation with Gulf & Western Industries in December 1975. As described in several chapters in this book, I'd done well with both the stock and warrants on several occasions. In that year the stock had moved up in an almost straight line, from 10 to 20. On the way up, I'd traded for a quick profit and sold in the 17–20 consolidation area.

Once again the chart looked strong. GW was still an UP stock, but, to be doubly sure, I reviewed the fundamentals. They were exciting. The per share earnings had risen from $1.50 in 1972 to $4.08 in 1975 and were estimated at $5.00 in 1976.

I checked the charts of other major diversified companies: Litton, Textron, ITT and Northwest Industries. They were UP, too. More important, the market was UP. The Dow Industrials were over 850 from a 1974 low of 578.

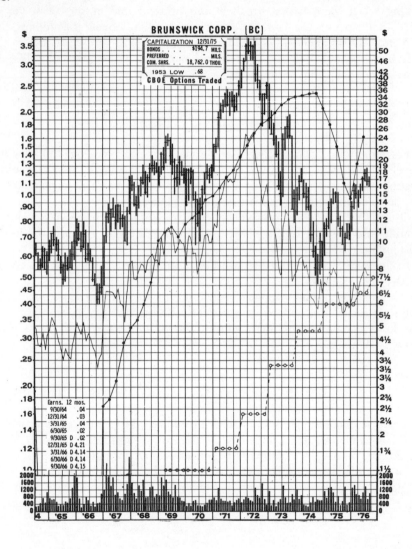

Now I turned to the long-term chart and saw two significant items:

1. Previous highs had been a long time ago: 20 in 1972 and 27 in 1967. Such long intervals between peaks are always bullish.

2. There was a strong V pattern, with heavier volume as the price advanced. The Big Boys were moving in.

The short-term chart showed the sharp upmove from 11 to 20, a short dip and another rise.

The buy signal came in January 1976 when the price rose, with the heaviest volume in four years, to 20½. This was a new high and, I felt, could mean a profit of 20 percent or more. I started buying at 20½.

The stock continued to move briskly with good volume and only minor dips. It hit a new high, then slipped back to 22, again with strong volume, and then bounced up again. This last move triggered my decision. It brought the stock near the top of the channel, and, soon broke through to another new high. I sold into strength at around the 26 level—a shade better than my 20 percent-profit target. Soon after, the downtrend started.

The stock dropped to 22. I knew that stop orders were being executed

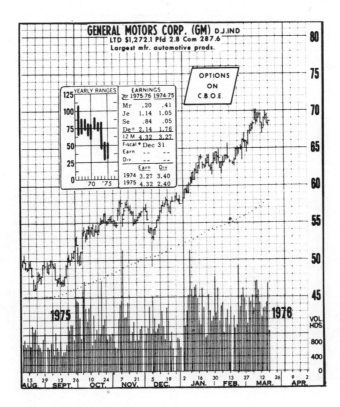

and that, for a few weeks anyway, there would be little chance of a rebound. It was time for every trader to get out and wait for new developments.

The chart sell signal was right. It predicted the future. By September, some six months later, the stock was down to around 15 (not as bad as it appears because of a stock dividend and a 5 for 4 stock split).

CHART FORMATION

When I see a favorable chart pattern, it directs me to stocks that I start to explore on a fundamental basis. If they prove to be of sufficient quality to be of interest to large investors and already have substantial institutional ownership (at least ten institutional owners as reported in Standard & Poor's Stock Guide), I place them on my Current List.

Then I watch the chart formations. There are scores of patterns used by technicians but I like to concentrate on those which, by my experience, work

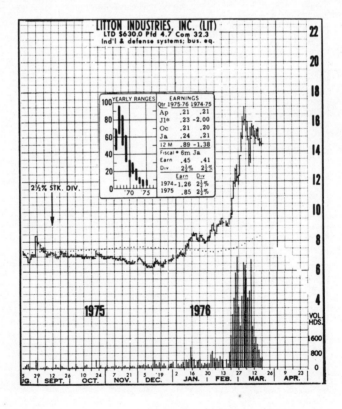

most of the time: Uptrends: 90 percent accurate; Upside breakouts: 70 percent correct; and Reversals of downtrendlines: 50 percent correct.

I have found that fancy formations—head & shoulders, wedges, island gaps, Prussian helmets, rounding bottoms, etc.—are seldom successful. Their signals are wrong more often than right. And their interpretation is difficult.

Here I am going to reemphasize my belief in the value of channels and breaks. Note how GM stock moved within a fairly narrow range during January and February 1976, broke down at 63½, just before a reversal for a sharp rise. The time to buy was at 64. If you were trading, you should have

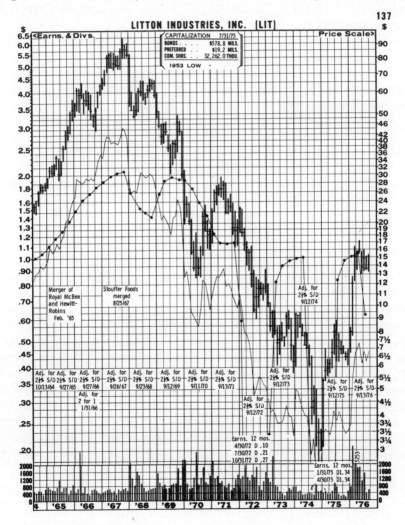

sold at 70. Thereafter the stock stayed in a consolidation area, and finally broke down through its channel.

Litton Industries is an even more dramatic illustration of how charts can be used to maximize profits and avoid losses. In 1976, LIT stock rose steadily, with moderate volume, until mid-February. The updrive started at about 8½, rocketed almost straight up, with heavy volume, to 12½. This was a 25 percent gain and a good spot to sell.

The stock then regrouped, fell a bit, with generally lower volume and, in late June, started up again to 17. By buying on the upswing, at about 14, the trader made 21 percent.

Note how the volume, at the bottom of the chart, showed when the institutions moved in as a herd.

There is no sure way to predict the length of any trend. Some uptrends last only a few weeks; others continue for months, and a rare few keep rising for years. You will make the greatest profits when you identify the uptrend early, but as the charts show, there can be plenty of room for profits after you are certain that the movement is for real.

My strategy is to buy only when the reward/risk ratio is in my favor: when the upside potential is great and the downside risk is small.

When you find a stock that meets these criteria, use the charts as a proving ground. Draw your channels and watch the uptrend. As long as that uptrendline continues (as with GM), do not sell unless one of the general sell signal rules is violated (Chapter 11).

BREAKOUTS

A breakout into a new high is a key buy signal. It shows a change in the equilibrium of the supply/demand equation. Someone is willing to pay an ever higher price. The greater the volume, the greater the interest by major investors.

Many technicians believe you should act immediately there's a breakout that involves double or triple tops (two or three consecutive highs) as with GM, at 45 in spring 1975 (page 57). I believe that such signals are useful, but not always valid. In fact, there are times when I feel it is wise to sell into these breakouts. There will be a lot of buyers, so I can be sure of getting rid of my stock quickly and probably profitably.

Blackman Strategy calls for buying on breakouts *only* when the market is strong and pounding up. This favorable situation does not occur often, perhaps five or six times over 12 months.

The best stocks to buy on breakouts are of two types:

1. Those reaching all-time highs: Halliburton

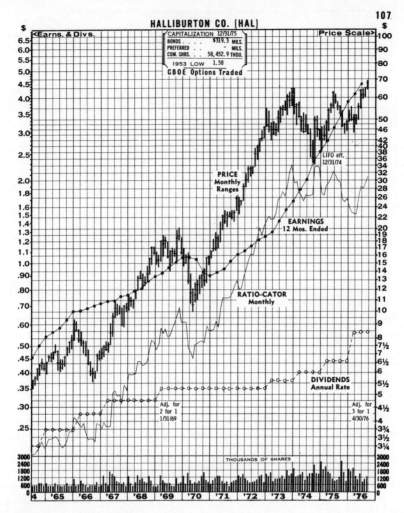

HALLIBURTON CO. (HAL)

CAPITALIZATION 12/31/75
BONDS . . . . $319.3 MILS.
PREFERRED . . – MILS.
COM. SHRS. . . 58,452.9 THOU.
1953 LOW 1.58
CBOE Options Traded

PRICE
Monthly
Ranges

EARNINGS
12 Mos. Ended

LIFO eff.
12/31/74

RATIO-CATOR
Monthly

DIVIDENDS
Annual Rate

Adj. for
2 for 1
1/31/69

Adj. for
3 for 1
4/30/76

THOUSANDS OF SHARES

2. Those reaching interim highs: ABC and Gulf & Western (see G&W Chart p. 199)

In both situations, you must use two charts: short and long term.

In mid-1974, Halliburton started up from a low of 35 and scored a fast gain to over 50. Then it went down below 40 in less than six months. In volume it was about the same under both swings. You had to be alert to catch the sudden shifts. HAL was a volatile stock.

The smart tactic was to play it safe—not to buy on the temporary up-swing from 36 to 40 but to wait for the stock to go up and show a clear reversal as it continued its strong upmove. On this basis, the earliest buying point was 43.

To be very safe, you should have skipped HAL entirely until mid-1974,

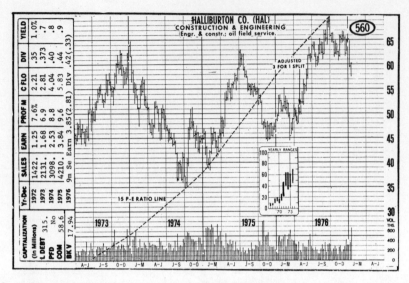

when the stock broke 51 and rose to a new high for the past 12 months. If you sold at the down break, around 62, you would have had a welcome profit—not as great as if you had been lucky in guessing the bottom, but you would have had fewer worries.

INTERIM HIGH

Another powerful configuration is an interim high: when the price of the stock moves into an area above that attained for many months, even though still below the all-time peak.

This happened with American Broadcasting Companies, Inc. (ABC), in March 1976 when the stock rose to 28. This was the highest value for about nine months. It was a get-ready signal. The stock dropped back to 26, then soared to 39 by July.

At this point, ABC was just short of its record price of 40, which had been reached in 1972–73. The stock did fall with the overall market, so it should have been sold for a profit. But with a new UP market, ABC was a strong candidate for another profitable move.

NOT ALL BREAKOUTS WORK

There are at least two situations where buying on breakouts is not usually successful: when the market is weak; and when the new high is made less than 12 months after the previous peak. Here's an example:

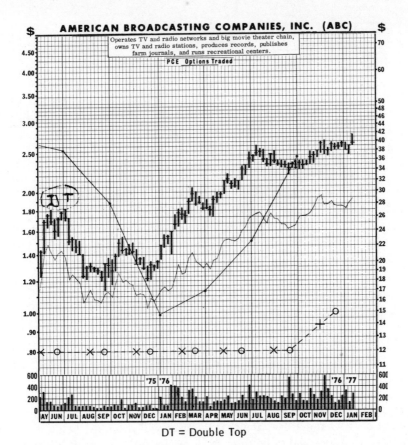

Operates TV and radio networks and big movie theater chain, owns TV and radio stations, produces records, publishes farm journals, and runs recreational centers.

PCE Options Traded

DT = Double Top

In spring 1974, Dow Chemical broke out at around 28, zipped to 34½, a new high. But then it fell back to 25. The overall market was poor and that new high came only nine months after the last top.

What happened was that people who had bought at a higher price in the last few months wanted to get even. When the stock rose close to their cost, in the low 30s, they started to sell and forced down the price.

General rule: Buy on a one-year-after-high breakout only when the market is very strong.

BUY INTO A BREAKDOWN?

Should you buy into a breakdown if you feel the stock is experiencing just a temporary dip? Sometimes. Trading is an art, not a science. Even when you try to be as analytical as possible, you must decide as an artist, not as a scientist. With experience you will occasionally break, or perhaps merely bend, a rule.

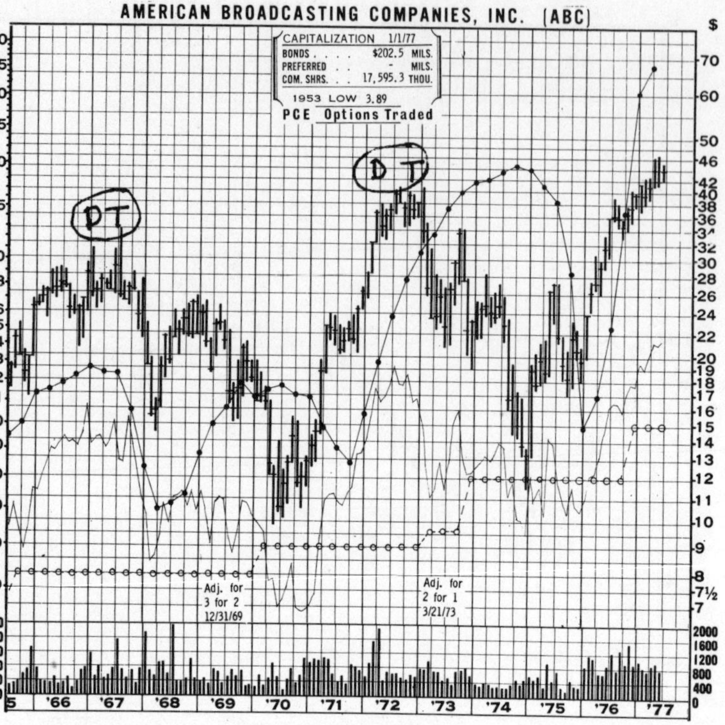

DT = Double Top

Many a time when I am trading a stock which, on a timing basis, is at the bottom of its channel, I notice that its price will drop just below the signal point. If it's a top-quality holding, such as General Motors, I do not become disturbed by a breakdown of a half a point or so. I keep tabs but do not act.

Most technicians will avoid purchase at this time because they regard this as a downside breakthrough. But I am not so dogmatic. I figure, What the hell. I'll take a chance that the stock will get back into its channel.

If I'm right (and I only do this with quality stocks), I will get an extra profit plus the impetus of buying below a key point. I would act only if I thought the risk was small: that the slide would not be more than 5 percent. Technicians who insist on going 100 percent by the book usually get some rude shocks. Successful trading takes experience. You must be flexible and cautious and, to a certain extent, be willing to play it by ear.

WAIT FOR CONFIRMATION

When the market is flat or moving down, I become wary about buying immediately on an upside breakout. I prefer to wait for confirmation. I have found that when a weak stock breaks upward in defiance of the overall market, there will usually be a pullback.

In most cases, a better time to buy is when the stock starts up again and forms an up trendline. By being patient, you can improve your timing and save some money. Still, the surest way to time profitable buying for the big breakout is when there's a major bull market.

A useful technique to spot a potential winner in such a situation is to start with a down trendline on your chart. Draw this by connecting the high points of the stock movement over the past year or so. (See Pittson.)

Now watch for the breakthrough, *on the upside,* of this channel. Again, this strategy works best with quality stocks, especially those which have declined because of temporary corporate or industry problems.

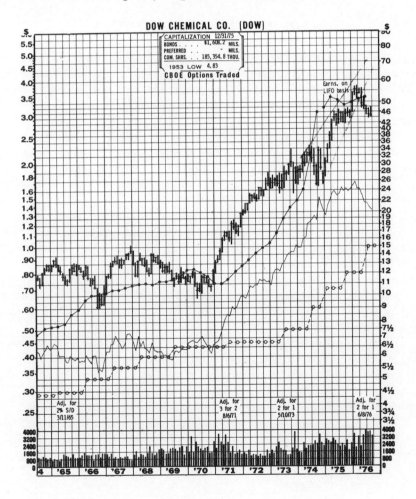

Take a look at Pittston in 1975 (page 52). The long-term chart showed a strong uptrend to an adjusted high of 22 in 1971–72. Then came a drop to below 10; a short, fast recovery; another shorter drop, and, finally, in March 1975, the start of an almost steady uptrend. The tip-off was the fact that the stock did not go down, the second time, as far as before. This could be a signal of the start of the up-drive. The trigger came with the breakout into an all-time high at 23. The market was good and the stock powered to 39 within three months!

This all-time high is a sure GO signal. Institutions, even those holding sizable blocks of stock, want to be in the act, and those which do not own shares will be stampeding.

BOTTOMS ARE HARD TO FIND

If technical analysis can enable you to pick a market or stock top, can it be used to spot a market/stock bottom? No. The chart will show support zones where the stop is supposed to occur, but I do not believe that technicians can pick exact bottoms. If they do, it's luck. At best, it's a guessing game.

Whenever someone tells me precisely where a market will bottom, I think of a piece of butter with a hot knife slicing through it—that's how easily supports are violated. And pay no heed to the theory that a bottom is reached when there's a sharp decline on ever lower volume. This seldom works out.

Realistically, catching the exact bottom is not important. If a stock is going to move up 40 percent or more, it's no great loss to miss the first 10 percent of the gain. You will be wiser, and safer, to wait for confirmation that the stock is in a real uptrend.

I know that there are able technicians who believe that a rounding bottom (where the configuration is like a bowl) is a sure way to catch a stock at a low price. In my experience, this is not usually a viable method. It works less than half the time.

To repeat: no matter how optimistic you feel, do not buy a stock when its price is declining and it is still out of favor. Wait for the UPmove. This must be preceded by a period of accumulation. A large enough group of investors must be convinced that the stock has reversed and is now ready to rise. That takes time. The best indication of a shift in sentiment is heavy volume.

One rare exception: when I am dealing with a quality stock which has a history of breaking up from a downswing. In such a situation, I may take a chance and buy early when the chart shows the start of a reversal of the downtrend and there's also a market rally.

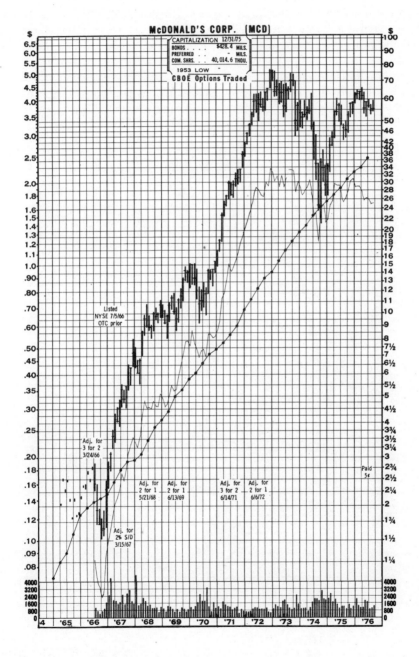

McDONALD'S CORP. (MCD)

CAPITALIZATION 12/31/75
BONDS . . . . $428.4 MILS.
PREFERRED . . - MILS.
COM. SHRS. . . 40,014.6 THOU.

1953 LOW
CBOE Options Traded

Listed
NYSE 7/5/66
OTC prior

Adj. for
3 for 2
3/24/66

Adj. for
2% S/D
3/15/67

Adj. for
2 for 1
5/21/68

Adj. for
2 for 1
6/13/69

Adj. for
3 for 2
6/14/71

Adj. for
2 for 1
6/6/72

Paid
5¢

McDonald's Corp. (MCD) fell to a new, interim low of around 22 in late 1974—this came after the heaviest volume in four years. The stock turned, fell back and, finally, moved up sharply to almost triple in value.

At the low I checked the fundamentals. When I found they were strong, I didn't wait for confirmation. I bought at 24 and took better than a 20 percent gain. After the second drop, I moved in again for an even greater profit.

I know that such a decision is only a guess, so I limit my commitment and watch carefully. If the stock slips back or moves sideways, I get ready to sell. Neither of these unfavorable actions occurred with MCD.

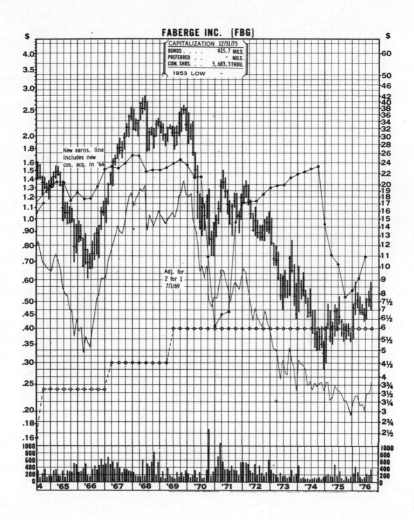

UNFAVORABLE CHART PATTERNS

Obviously there are unfavorable chart patterns: downtrends and downside breakouts. They can be used to signal short selling in a bear market, but, for my money, they are seldom worthwhile at any other time. The alert trader has already sold—at the first sure sign of a reversal of the UPtrend that caused the original purchase.

A good illustration of this point is the Head & Shoulders (H&S) chart. These are popular with many technicians. This portrays three successive rallies and reactions with the second reaching a higher point than either of the others. The first and last rallies are the shoulders: the center is the head.

According to "rules" of technical analysis, the sell signal comes when the third rally fails to equal the second peak. The major trend has come to an end. To be sure, you are supposed to wait until there's a break down through the neckline—the line drawn between the two early lows.

Honestly now, isn't this stupid, useless and expensive? You are supposed to lose money, then wait for a comeback, lose more money, hope for a comeback, etc. The time to sell was when the first up trendline was violated at the top of the channel, *before* the first decline started. You might have gone back at the interim low, repeated the profitable sale, etc. But why in the world should anyone, in his right mind, hold a loser in hopes of a favorable future chart pattern?

Note: H&S patterns can occur both straight up (see chart on page 72) or reversed.

DOWN-DOWN-DOWN STOCKS

The most unfavorable chart pattern of all is that of a DOWN stock. You don't have to be a chart expert to understand the Eastern Air Lines (EAL) configuration. If you held on through dismal 1969 and 1970 in hopes that the stock would get back to the price you paid, you should have heeded the most important signal of all: the breakthrough to a long-term low of 11. This was below the 1970 nadir and the 13 depth of 1964. If you had sold, you would have saved yourself a further loss of over eight points.

Study this chart as if you owned the stock at the time. Note how it really plummeted after that second signal in early 1973. Most of the time the volume was miniscule and changed little with the upmoves in 1975. Obviously, few investors were interested.

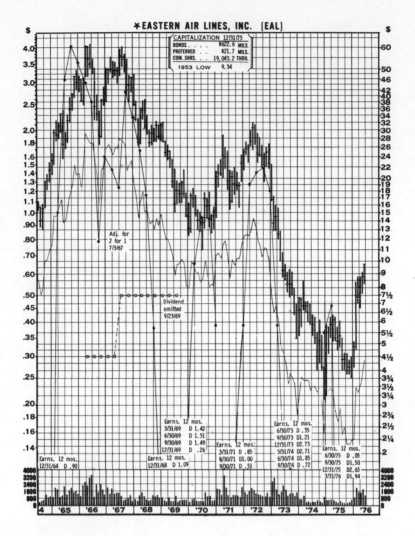

✱EASTERN AIR LINES, INC. (EAL)

CAPITALIZATION 12/31/75
BONDS . . . . $622.6 MILS.
PREFERRED . . $21.7 MILS.
COM. SHRS. . . 19,043.2 THOU.

1953 LOW   9.34

A daring speculator might have gambled for a gain after the January 1976 rise above 5, but by this time EAL had such a heavy debt and deficit that it was no longer a quality stock.

If you had been foolish enough to hang on in the early 1970s, the time to sell was after the 32 top when the uptrend channel was broken.

When it's a DOWN stock, sell for the fastest, smallest loss you can. *Do not continue to dream of a comeback.*

CHARTS AND INSIDE INFORMATION

When you become familiar with charts, you will find that "inside informa-tion" will confirm what the charts have already indicated. This was the case, in mid-January 1976, with Chrysler. The chart showed a definite upmove. There was no news to cause this.

But a month later one of my RRs learned from a friendly bank fund manager that an automobile company official had said that the first-quarter profit would be close to $1.00 a share. Coming after a deficit year, this was good news. But the chart had already flagged the news.

OTHER TOOLS OF TECHNICAL ANALYSIS

There are other technical tools that can be used to determine the direction of the market and the trends of specific stocks. Some of these are valuable as background and confirmation, but none of them have a fraction of the importance of price action. In the stock market, price determines everything. With Blackman Strategy, the chart is the surest, most convenient and most effective reflection of price movement. It records the tape, so you have truth piled on truth: an unbeatable combination.

8. How to Read the Financial Pages for Profit

With Blackman Strategy, you must keep alert and watch what's happening in the stock market and business world. This means reading the financial pages carefully. Here's an outline of my schedule.

During the week I watch the daily tables that report stocks/bonds activity. Over the weekend I check the weekly and group action. In both cases I refer back to the week or two before. I want to catch trends and discover those stocks which are of interest to major investors. I concentrate on high quality and well-known companies, and skip those which are one-day wonders. What I am looking for is a base from which to utilize my charts.

I always look for well-known companies whose names appear for the first time in many months on the New Highs and Most Active Stock lists. When they are among the leaders more than once in a short span of time, I go to the charts and check them out.

When any stock becomes popular and shows an ever higher price, it's a possible line-driver. My philosophy is to BUY HIGH—SELL HIGHER. I keep alert if the volume continues strong even though there may be down swings, especially in the closing price. I've learned that, while most of the in-day transactions may be at rising prices, there will often be a dip at day's end. This creates the impression that the stock did not move up that day. Always check the daily highs and lows of stocks you own or are considering buying. You may catch an uptrend that doesn't appear in the closing statistics.

Pay special attention when the same stock closes at ever lower prices. Probably, the Big Boys are selling. If the daily drop is more than one point (except on a high-valued issue), it is an almost certain indication that the institutions are moving out and are not overly concerned with the prices they get.

On the financial pages, I keep watch on:

Most Active (Stocks). This list shows the ten stocks, all traded on the NYSE, that accounted for the greatest volume. Generally this list includes only issues which traded more than 100,000 shares that day, 500,000 for the week.

This is a good starting point for a list of stocks to watch. It illustrates my strategy of following the leaders: the institutional investors without whose support there could be no such heavy demand. These are the issues which the Big Boys feel are capable of scoring significant gains. Their activity attracts other institutions as well as traders, so there is likely to be a strong uptrend when it's an UP stock.

New York Stock Exchange Issues

CONSOLIDATED TRADING

MARKET INDICATORS — MONDAY, OCTOBER 31, 1977

N.Y.S.E. Index

	High	Low	Last	Chg
Index	50.75	50.65	50.65	-0.12
Industrial	54.43	54.31	54.31	-0.18
Transport	37.90	37.78	37.83	-0.07
Utility	39.69	39.63	39.64	+0.05
Finance	52.20	52.06	52.06	-0.08

Up-Down Share Volume

	Advanced	Declined
NYSE	6,292,930	7,227,96C
AMEX	704,530	490,490

Odd-Lot Trading

Purchases of 121,000 shares; sales of 202,944 shares including 1,358. shares sold short.

S. & P. Index

	High	Low	Close	Chg.
400 Indust	102.50	101.21	101.77	-0.32
20 Transpt	12.87	12.67	12.76	-0.04
40 Utilities	53.70	53.02	53.28	.....
40 Financial	10.89	10.76	10.79	-0.04
500 Stocks	93.03	91.83	92.34	-0.27

Amex Index

High	Low	Close	Chg.
113.04	112.86	113.02	+0.16

NASDAQ Index

Index	Close	Chg.	Week Ago	Month Ago
Composite	97.52	+0.03	97.89	closed
Indust	100.01	+0.05	100.18	closed
Financl	99.99	unch	100.55	closed
Insurance	105.65	-0.01	106.41	closed
Utilities	95.86	-0.08	96.36	closed
Banks	93.60	+0.15	93.61	closed
Transport	93.46	+0.17	94.09	closed

Dow Jones Stock Averages

	Open	High	Low	Close	Chg
30 Industrials	821.47	824.93	813.93	818.35	- 4.33
20 Transport	205.54	207.68	204.23	206.08	+ 0.30
15 Utilities	109.47	110.13	108.78	109.04	- 0.36
65 Stocks	280.48	282.20	278.26	279.86	- 0.90

Consolidated Trading for Amex Issues Most Active

Name	Vol	Last	Net Chg
HouOilM	51,000	28	- ⅜
Baruch Fost	35,300	3⅝	+ ⅞
Susquehan	33,800	7⅜	+ ⅛
Cdn Homstd	22,700	7½	.....
Syntex Corp	21,300	16⅜	- ¼
Hycel Inc	20,600	5⅜	.....
AlldArt Ind	20,400	1⅜	- ⅛
TotalPtl NA	20,200	8¼	- ⅛
SCE 4.08pf	20,000	12⅜	- ⅛
Comodr Intl	18,700	13	- ¾

Amex Market Diary

	Today	Prev. day
Advanced	286	318
Declined	265	250
Unchanged	308	268
Total issues	859	836
New 1977 highs	7	5
New 1977 lows	20	14

O.T.C. Most Active

Name	Volume	Bid	Asked	Chg.
DeBeer	139,300	3⅜	3½	-5-32
AnheusB	129,700	22	22½	- ⅜
MgtAssis	94,400	7⅞	8⅜	+ ¼
MonuCp	93,300	19¾	20¼	.....
Daylin	91,400	1½	1⅝	.....
GvtEmp	61,500	6¾	7⅛	+ ¼
KebaOG	55,300	1¼	1⅜	.....
BrwTom	55,100	41¾	42½	-1
AnglSA	51,500	3 5-16	3 7-16	-3-16
MCI Com	49,100	2 13-16	3 1-16	-3-16

O.T.C. Market Diary

Advanced	422
Declined	275
Unchanged	1,846
Total issues	2,543
New highs	35
New lows	23
Total sales	6,210,800

Consolidated Trading for N.Y.S.E. Issues

Changes – Up

	Name	Last	Chg		Pct.
1	Arlen Rlty	2⅞	+ ⅜	Up	15.0
2	UMET Tr	2⅜	+ ¼	Up	11.8
3	Frigitronc	10⅛	+ ⅞	Up	9.5
4	CocaBtg NY	9	+ ¾	Up	9.1
5	LawterCh	9	+ ¾	Up	9.1
6	Bayuk Cig	8⅞	+ ⅝	Up	7.6
7	Dymo Ind	13⅛	+ ⅞	Up	7.1
8	Alberto Cul	7⅝	+ ½	Up	7.0
9	Republic Cp	7⅞	+ ½	Up	6.8
10	ContCopp pf	12½	+ ¾	Up	6.4
11	Bobbie Brks	4¼	+ ¼	Up	6.3
12	CLC Am	4¼	+ ¼	Up	6.3
13	UnPark Min	2⅛	+ ⅛	Up	6.3
14	USRlty Inv	4¼	+ ¼	Up	6.3
15	Allen Grp	17½	+ 1	Up	6.1

Changes – Down

	Name	Last	Chg		Pct.
1	HudsBay B	12½	- 1½	Off	10.7
2	NtMedCare	22½	- 2¼	Off	9.1
3	Nat Homes	2¾	- ¼	Off	8.3
4	Colum Pict	17	- 1⅜	Off	7.5
5	EsterlinCp	6⅛	- ½	Off	7.5
6	RoyCr Cola	16⅞	- 1⅜	Off	7.5
7	ContCppfB	54½	- 4¼	Off	7.2
8	Union Corp	5	- ⅜	Off	7.0
9	NoAmMtg	3⅝	- ¼	Off	6.5
10	BayColPrp	2	- ⅛	Off	5.9
11	CarlingOKe	2	- ⅛	Off	5.9
12	Telex Corp	2	- ⅛	Off	5.9
13	Tobin Pack	6⅛	- ⅜	Off	5.8
14	Appld Mag	2¼	- ⅛	Off	5.3
15	CentrnData	20¼	- 1⅛	Off	5.3

N.Y.S.E. Issues—Volume by Exchanges

Markets	Shares
NYSE	17,070,000
Pacific	584,200
Midwest	805,700
NASD	877,900
Boston	108,900
Cinci	161,000
Amex	1,500
Phila	348,100
Other	10,500
Total	19,967,800

Most Active

Name	Vol	Last	Net Chg
VetcoInc	425,800	23⅞	+ ⅛
IntTelTel	328,400	29⅞	.....
IntT&T pfN	219,300	36⅞	- ⅛
Brit Pet	219,200	16¼	+ ¼
StdOil Cal	199,600	38¾	- ¼
GlobeUni	176,500	45⅛	+1⅜
Citicorp	172,000	22⅜	.....
Colum Pict	169,300	17	-1⅜
Dow Ch	165,900	28⅞	.....
Dr Pepper	161,900	14⅞	+ ⅛
Weyerhsr	151,500	26	+ ½
CocaBtg NY	135,800	9	+ ¾
Zale Corp	131,400	16	- ⅛
AmTT	120,000	59⅝	+ ⅛
Texaco Inc	117,900	27⅜	- ½

Market Diary

	Today	Prev. day
Advanced	658	838
Declined	698	531
Unchanged	503	484
Total issues	1859	1853
New 1977 highs	14	9
New 1977 lows	49	46

Dollar Leaders

Name	Tot ($1000)	Sales (hds)	Last
IBM	$15,332	594	257¼
Vetco	$10,219	4258	23⅞
IntTT	$9,934	3284	29⅞
IntTT pf	$8,086	2193	36⅞
GlobeU	$7,920	1765	45⅛
StOilCl	$7,734	1996	38¾
ATT	$7,125	1200	59⅝
GnMot	$6,893	1025	67¼
EsKod	$5,081	961	52¾
DigitalEq	$5,022	1110	44⅞
Dow Ch	$4,769	1659	28⅞
ProctG	$4,340	523	82⅞
AlconLb	$4,222	1059	39⅞
JohnJn	$4,174	567	73⅝
duPont	$4,101	363	112½

N.Y.S.E. Volume Comparisons

Day's Sales	17,070,000
Friday's Sales	18,050,000
Year Ago	18,390,000
1977 to Date	4,327,703,992
1976 to Date	4,444,502,518

The beginning of this drive already may have taken place, but usually there is still a lot of potential, especially with stocks that are newcomers to this Most Active list. You cannot expect to buy at the bottom or sell at the top. What you want to do is to concentrate on the main movement, which I call the "meat and potatoes."

Judge each stock against the action of the overall market. It's important when the price movement is opposite that of the averages; it's *very* important if this trend continues with heavy volume. Somebody knows something.

With all Most Active stocks, be realistic. You must relate the volume and the corporation and the overall market. You can expect General Motors and Exxon to be listed frequently because they have such a tremendous number of outstanding shares. Be alert when the list includes the names of smaller corporations when they are of high quality.

For example, on Monday, September 27, 1976, the volume of the NYSE was 14.5 million shares, a fair-to-good day then. The 206,400 shares of Polaroid were eye-catching, as this was a stock that had been unpopular for several years. It was also significant that this was the second time, in less than a week, that PRD had been heavily traded, at ever higher prices.

Remember: this is only a starting point for further investigation!

Pay special attention, on the Most Active list and on the general stock tables, to the types of stocks with big moves. In down markets, high-quality glamours are usually slow to move with the market. The averages will drop for several days before you see a sharp break by institutional favorites: IBM down 5 points, Teledyne off 6, etc. In many cases, such action may signal the end of a temporary drop in the market.

WATCH INDUSTRY ACTION

Another thing to watch is the appearance of several stocks of the same industry: in this case, utilities: Texas Utilities, Middle South Utilities and AT&T.

WHAT HAPPENED TO POLAROID?

When Polaroid hit 45 in late September 1976, this was an important signal. This was the highest point the stock had reached in two years. The charts indicated that, with a good market, PRD could go to 60, the point at which the last major decline had started. Thereafter there had been a free fall to 14, so it was possible, even probable, that the stock could run up just as easily.

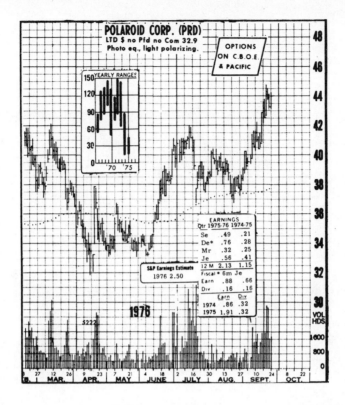

The fundamentals were good. Earnings had been improving steadily. The company had no long-term debt. Its new cameras were doing well, while Kodak's had run into production troubles and an unfavorable court ruling in England. Some of the smart money appeared to be moving out of EK into PRD.

My belief that this could be a line-drive stock was reinforced when I saw that the historical action had been so sharp. The stock moved almost in a straight line, up and down, with almost no consolidation periods.

The problem was that the overall market was unfavorable. Except for an occasional spurt, the trend was down.

This hesitation proved to be wise. The third-quarter earnings were not as high as some analysts anticipated. The stock slid, with the overall market, below 37. But it did not break down through the channel line. PRD was still on the top of my Watch list. I was ready for a heavy commitment when the chart showed a renewal of the favorable trend.

Sad to say, there was no confirmed upmove. Together with other ex-glamour stocks, PRD kept falling and did not warrant interest until it was under 30 and then only with a confirmed uptrend.

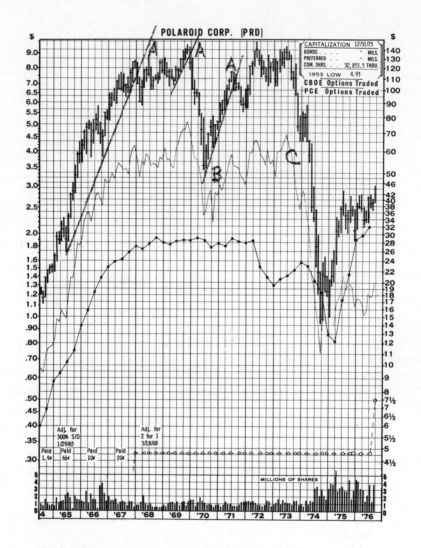

POLAROID CORP. (PRD)

A = break in uptrend line, becoming a DOWN stock

B = break in downtrend line, becoming an UP stock

C = break through resistance point, which was previous interim low

Market Averages. These show the trend of the overall stock market and of a few major stock groups. These are important points of reference which are widely used by analysts and money managers.

The best known and most widely used is the Dow Jones Industrial Average. This shows the price action of the stocks of 30 major corporations and, generally speaking, reflects what is happening to the types of stocks favored by institutional investors. Some people prefer the NYSE Index or the Standard & Poor's Industrial Average. By and large, all averages parallel each other.

On this same Monday, September 27, 1976, the Dow Industrial Average closed at 1,013.13, up 3.82 points from the closing price of the previous trading day, Friday, September 24. This figure was used on many published charts, so my next step was to check the trendline of the chart and watch for breakthroughs and patterns.

I find the other averages useful for confirmation and data on specific groups: Transportation for railroad and airline stocks; Utilities for electric and gas companies; Financial for banks and savings and loans.

I just glance at the AMEX (American Stock Exchange) index and NASDAQ (National Association of Securities Dealers Automated Quotations—the over-the-counter market) index. Their stocks seldom meet top-quality standards.

The same goes for Changes Up and Down. These statistics are interesting, but usually involve low-priced stocks where a small dollar move can make a large percentage change. Once in a while, of course, these will flash some ideas worth checking.

Dollar Leaders. By definition, this table favors the high-priced stocks. On this date, September 27, IBM was at 286¾ and Du Pont at 129¼. Generally these data reflect institutional commitments: here, $37.5 million investments in just three companies: IBM, GM and Ford. That's a lot of money that will not be available for other stocks.

Highs and Lows. This contains the names of all stocks which, on the previous day, exceeded the previous peaks or depths of the current year.

I look at this every day. It's a good place for leads and ideas. I keep copies of this report for a week or two to spot trends of industry groups.

The HIGH list is especially valuable in a weak market because it spotlights those issues which were able to advance on their own. *I believe that no stock can score a major advance without appearing on this list.*

Advances/Declines. These are shown in the Market Diary. This reports what the main body of stocks, not the selected few that make up the averages, is doing. On this day there were 827 advances and 568 declines. This was a sizable improvement over the previous trading day, when 639 stocks went up and 737 dropped.

The new highs and lows also show what is happening across the board. In an uncertain market, when the averages are down, the fact that a number of stocks hit new highs is a generally bullish sign. But not always. These figures must be taken over more than one day.

Up Stock in a Down Day/Week. I find this a valuable guide to future stock action. When any stock bucks the market fairly consistently, some investors must know something favorable.

This can be a do-it-yourself project. When the overall market is slipping or moving sideways, I take time to run down the full tables of trading on the NYSE. I circle the name of every stock which advanced a full point or more. On Sunday, I do this for the week with a two-point upmove.

These rises are like charts. They indicate possibly popular stocks—those which some buyers are so eager to acquire that they are willing to bid up the price in an overall downtrend.

When I have transcribed the list, I divide the stocks into industry groups and then check performance in *Barron's* or the Associated Press index. Now I have a base from which to learn what's happening and where there's likely to be favorable action.

CHECKING GROUP AVERAGES

The market action of groups of stocks can be followed in two places:

1. *The weekly report by Associated Press.* This is published in some Saturday and many Sunday papers. It shows the average net change, in percentages, for common stocks traded in each group the previous week. This is a handy frame of reference for your present and prospective holdings.

2. *Group Stock Averages in* Barron's. This publication is on the newsstand on Sunday and delivered by mail on Monday.

These data are more complete. They show the highs and lows for the year, the group averages for the past week and the week before, and the percentage of change.

Using all of this information, I concluded that the strongest groups for the week ending September 23, 1976 were: grocery chains, + 5.43%; steel and iron, + 4.58%; tobacco, + 3.60%; and building materials, + 3.51%.

The three weakest groups (to be avoided unless you are selling short) were: farm equipment, − 5.17%; banks, − 2.59%; and retailers, − 1.11%.

No one week is enough to force action. Wait for confirmation of trends.

BARRON'S GROUP STOCK AVERAGES

1976 High-a	Low-a		Sept. 23	Sept. 16	% change
180.24	121.61	Aircraft manufacturing ....H	185.77	180.24	+ 3.07
113.13	72.59	Air transport	93.44	92.44	+ .65
105.84	82.81	Automobiles ....H	107.11	103.12	+ 3.87
169.60	128.31	Automobile equipment	165.98	164.22	+ 1.07
337.99	264.72	Banks	301.04	309.05	— 2.59
212.54	163.15	Bldg mat and equipment	197.16	190.47	+ 3.51
401.83	337.65	Chemicals	368.00	363.82	+ 1.15
30.42	27.94	Closed-End Invest	30.21	29.57	+ 2.16
928.63	789.06	Drugs ....H	938.09	914.16	+ 2.62
438.78	348.32	Electrical equip	422.83	419.26	+ .85
599.50	426.42	Farm equipment	539.62	569.02	— 5.17
347.17	300.94	Foods and beverages	345.90	345.68	+ .06
398.06	196.44	Gold mining	222.11	224.83	— 1.21
341.06	289.10	Grocery chains	332.96	315.82	+ 5.43
169.14	139.58	Instalment financing ....H	173.66	168.06	+ 3.33
750.82	568.23	Insurance ....H	767.84	743.06	+ 3.33
400.61	345.96	Liquor	361.46	352.81	+ 2.45
87.72	64.09	Machine tools	78.05	76.73	+ 1.72
75.27	53.00	Machinery (heavy)	72.10	71.30	+ 1.12
402.90	312.41	Motion pictures	321.67	325.80	— 1.27
166.76	128.81	Non-Ferrous Metals	154.06	151.20	+ 1.89
2,531.77	2,058.12	Office equipment ....H	2,537.21	2,531.77	+ .21
428.85	349.43	Oil ....H	432.54	424.17	+ 1.97
126.57	117.42	Packing	123.27	121.79	+ 1.21
311.30	245.76	Paper	286.23	289.89	+ 1.90
165.43	119.60	Railroad equipment ....H	168.34	165.43	+ 1.76
644.19	533.82	Retail merchandise	558.03	564.32	— 1.11
391.59	343.88	Rubber	379.50	368.06	+ 3.11
330.40	259.20	Steel and iron	296.84	283.85	+ 4.58
259.90	190.35	Television	247.80	241.38	+ 2.66
274.80	215.69	Textiles	225.23	220.39	+ 2.20
148.43	130.18	Tobacco	143.21	138.23	+ 3.60
1,007.71	907.98	Dow-Jones Industrials ....H	1,010.80	987.95	+ 2.31
229.69	185.06	Dow-Jones Transportation Cos.	221.34	217.71	+ 1.67
96.82	84.93	Dow-Jones Utilities ....H	98.16	96.82	+ 1.38

a-1976 highs and lows through preceding week. In this table Thursday closings used in Dow-Jones Averages. H-New high.

Change in Components: Farm Equipment: Deere & Company; 2-for-1 stock split, new multiplier is 48.

	Last week	Prev. week	Last year
Member trading, week ended Sept. 10, 1976			
% total	22.56	23.88	23.61
Purchases, th shs	15,884.1	17,534.6	16,737.9
Sales, th shs-z	15,600.2	19,574.4	14,293.5
Short sales, th shs	3,663.6	4,732.9	3,124.6
Specialists, th shs	2,149.3	2,686.8	1,774.5
Tot short sls, th shs	4,483.0	5,687.7	4,443.1

Short Sales. The best source for these bearish professional transactions is *Barron's,* in the back pages under the column "Week's Market Statistics." Short sales are valuable in judging the strength of the market.

This published report is three weeks old but still useful. It shows short sales by NYSE specialists—the brokers who are in a position to have information before it becomes generally known. They are market makers who help to provide liquidity. Their activities do not represent a significant percentage of total NYSE transactions, but, to prosper, they must have a keen sense of market direction. When they are bearish, they sell short. When they are bullish they cover their positions.

To plan your trading strategy, find the ratio of the specialists' sales to total short sales:

1. Get the total short sales for the week: 4,483,000
2. Check the specialist short sales: 2,149,300
3. Divide (2) by (1): 2.1 by 4.5 = 48%
4. To find the market trend, compare the percentage with that of the previous week: 5.687.6 divided by 2,686.8 = 47%

This 48 percent is a neutral figure and shows only a slight change from the week before. When the ratio is 40 percent or less, the market outlook is bullish. At 60 percent or higher, the prospects are bearish and it's time to sell. On the basis of this week's figure, stand pat.

IMPORTANT NEWS

Watch the financial pages for news stories that affect the industries and stocks in which you are interested. The best news is when new executives put their money where their jobs are. This sets up two chances for profits: short-term when the stock runs up a few points on the announcement; long-term on the belief that the new boss (or bosses) can boost profits and make the stock attractive to major investors.

The news is most effective with an already profitable company, such as

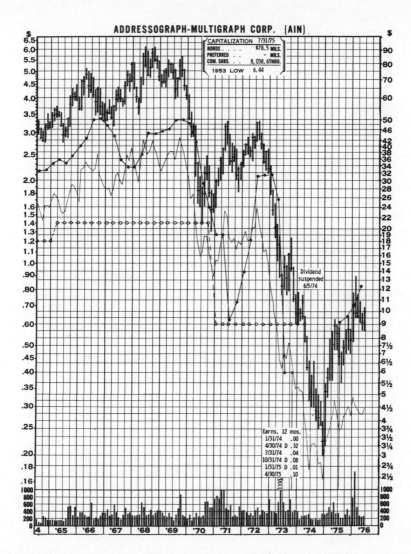

ADDRESSOGRAPH-MULTIGRAPH CORP. (AIN)

CAPITALIZATION 7/31/75
BONDS . . . $78.5 MILS.
PREFERRED . . — MILS.
COM. SHRS. . . 8,038.6 THOU.
1953 LOW 6.44

Dividend
suspended
6/5/74

Earns. 12 mos.
1/31/74 .00
4/30/74 D .32
7/31/74 .04
10/31/74 D .08
1/31/75 D .01
4/30/75 .10

Addressograph-Multigraph Corp. (AIN). In the fall of 1976 it was announced that Roy L. Ash, one of the founders of Litton Industries and a former head of the U.S. Office of Management and Budget, had bought 300,000 shares of AIN for $2.7 million and had been elected chairman and chief executive officer of this manufacturer of business equipment.

The stock ran up from 9 to 11⅞, then dropped back in a generally down market. But from personal contacts I knew that many institutional researchers were checking AIN—just as I did.

The charts showed that this stock could be poised for a line drive:

• The support level was 10, the price at which the stock had sold before its dividend was suspended in 1974;

• The 11⅝ price was a seven-month high, so a strong market could carry the stock past 13½ to 20;

• The chart showed a strong V formation with a sharp, rapid rise from the 1974 low of 3. This indicated the stock could still be a powerhouse.

The fundamentals were also good:

• The company had reported a rising profit for the last two quarters—reversing a downward trend

• Debt was only 27% of capitalization so loans for acquisitions would not be onerous

• Working capital was an adequate $150 million and rising

• Capitalization was small: about 8 million shares

• There were already 21 institutional shareholders

Now I tried to think like my friends, the professional portfolio managers. With all these favorable factors, plus the acquisition skill and management ability of Mr. Ash, AIN *had* to be on the institutional Futures list. I felt that with some profit improvement, one or two acquisitions, and an UP market, this stock could triple in a couple of years.

With such a potential, strengthened by Ash's willingness to invest his own money, almost every fund would have to buy some shares and many would move in with large purchases.

Whether it was time to buy depended on one's pocketbook and market conditions. Wealthy people could start acquiring shares and wait. Personally I preferred to keep checking the charts. By July, AIN was over 15.

What about bad news? Of course, this can affect investments and investment strategy. But, except for the few unpredictable events (disasters such as hurricanes, plane crashes, etc.) the bad news has usually been signaled by the charts months before the governmental ban, antitrust suit or corporate reorganization is announced.

CHECK YOUR OWN RECORDS

The best proof of the success of the Blackman Strategy is your own investment record. Get out your old tax returns and review the stocks you bought and sold with the charts.

I'll wager that most of your profits came from UP stocks in UP groups in UP markets. Vice versa for your losses. You can always learn from your mistakes.

OTHER INDICATORS

Other data/techniques that have limited use with the Blackman Strategy but are popular with some technical analysts include:

Moving Averages. These show the market or stock action over a period of time: 30 days, 60 days, 200 days, etc. They are formed by plotting the closing price each day and dropping the oldest price; i.e., adding the final price of the 30th day and dropping that of Day 1.

These can be shown as charts or figures. To get an arithmetical Moving Average, divide the total by the number of days.

The chart is then compared with a standard average, Dow Jones or S&P, to show differences in market action. With industry groups, I use a 200-day Moving Average plotted against the Dow Industrials. This quickly shows when divergent trends are developing, and it is useful in catching shifts in investor sentiment.

Interest Rates. All markets depend on the cost and availability of money. When money is plentiful and cheap (when interest rates are low), the stock market will move up. Conversely, when money is expensive and tight (when interest rates are rising), the stock market tends to go down. See for yourself in the charts of the New York and London Exchanges in Chapter 5.

If you really want to make money in the stock market, try to set aside 15 minutes every morning to read the financial pages. If you cannot do this regularly, make it a weekly assignment: with your big city Sunday paper, the Monday *Wall Street Journal* and the weekly edition of *Barron's*. These will provide the basic information you need as background for reading charts.

9.   Catching Shifts in Industry Trends

The stock market runs in cycles, and so do industry groups and individual stocks. These swings, up and down, are best identified in charts, as you can see for yourself.

Take the Dow Jones Industrial Average (page 112). The overall movement has always been up: from around 255 in 1953 to 1,014 in September 1976. Between times there have been dips, some small, short and insignificant; many large and profitable; or, on down swings, devastating: from 437 in 1958 to 735 in 1961, down to 536, up almost steadily to 995 in 1966; then down to 744, up to 985 in 1968, down to 631 in 1970, up to 1,052 in 1973, down to 578 in 1974 and, in 1976, over 1,000 again.

The swings in stock groups have been even more dramatic. With industrial-machinery stocks, there was a long up drive from about 60 in 1966 to 110 in 1968, then down to 60 in 1970. There was a fairly steady up drive to a high of 140 in 1973; a sharp, sudden dip in the 1974 recession, and a rapid recovery in 1975, a short reversal and another gain to the 140 level. This was followed by a downside break, which, at this writing, is still continuing. The end of another cycle has been reached.

These group down shifts are often signaled by the chart of individual stocks: in this case, Ingersoll-Rand. In July 1976 the stock dropped sharply. Two months later came the explanation: IR's profits would be down, from the $6.42 per share of 1975 to an estimated $6.20 in 1976.

The utility average provides even better proof of the cyclical trends which, of course, reflect investor sentiment. After moving to a new high of 160 in 1965, the Dow Jones Utility Average went into an almost steady decline. Despite a slight upmove in 1971, these stocks held within a narrow range, 130 to 100, and, as the result of the energy crisis, dropped deeply in

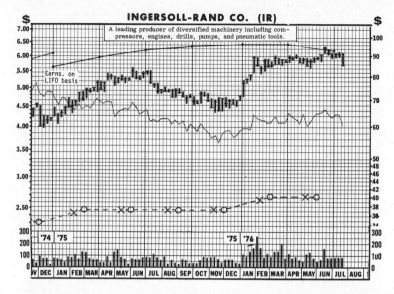

1973 and 1974 to below 60. This was a little less than one third of the previous high value.

The decline of electric and gas company stocks lasted about ten years. When Wall Street sours on an industry, the unpopularity can continue for a long, long time. The primary reason why investors owned AT&T, Pacific Gas & Electric, Public Service Electric & Gas, etc., was for the ample dividends.

But when utility stocks do start to move, they can be red-hot. You may never find a fast-swinging Polaroid, but with a line-drive utility stock, gains can be more certain.

With utilities, I shoot for a 10 percent profit. I am not afraid to invest heavily because I know the risk is limited. Common stocks of a quality utility are as safe as any investment I know.

The time to buy utilities is when interest rates are dropping. Electric, gas and telephone companies borrow huge sums for expansion, so they benefit from the lower cost of money. Trading profits can be quick, especially when the institutions move in with their large purchases.

With utilities, I pay attention to block trades: 50,000 or more shares. And I take quick profits. With American Electric Power, I made my money in just two days!

NONCYCLICALS

Noncyclicals are groups that are not affected severely by the costs of money or capital spending. Drug stocks are a good example. Generally these

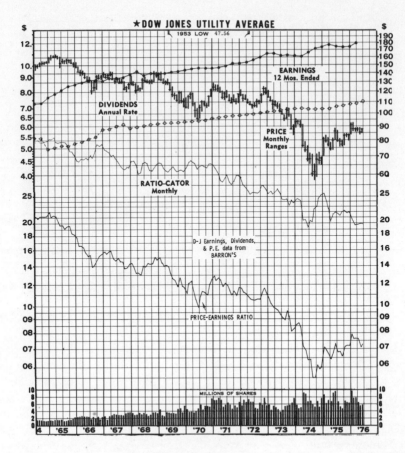

companies continue to report high profits year in and year out. Their shares are set back by bad news or overvaluation—as in 1973.

Note that chart line: almost straight up from a base of 80 in 1964 to over 260 in 1973. Over those years, drug stocks included a number of line-drive opportunities.

I believe they will again. In fact, the drug group up drive started in late July 1976. This was the time I took a first look at the drug industry and began to target specific stocks. My reasoning was this:

1. The cyclicals were through. Institutions might not start selling steels and machinery manufacturers, but they would not be buying. With lower volume, these stocks would, at best, hold their position; and, as I have stressed, this is equivalent to a loss position under Blackman Strategy.

2. The Big Boys would move into more dependable groups such as drugs. Fundamental research confirmed the industry's future: earnings were expected to grow at a rate of 12 percent a year. Such a gain may not be as

sensational as the 25 percent profit jumps reported by some industrial firms but it's a lot better than can be expected for the economy as a whole.

Other factors: (a) Drugs were among the hardest-hit stocks in the sharp decline experienced by many glamour-growth stocks in 1973–74 and had been slow to rebound; (b) Institutional holdings were down to 3.2 percent of total portfolios from 9 percent at the end of 1974. *By logical criteria, the selling of drug stocks was over and buying was beginning.*

With that background, I started checking charts of individual drug companies. In the next few months, I saw Abbott Laboratories hit an eight-year high; Bristol-Myers flirt with an all-time peak; and Merck start to move out

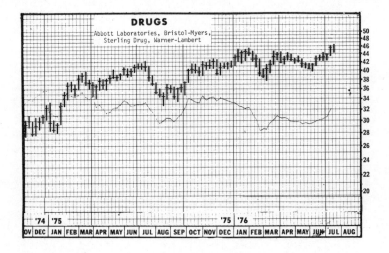

DRUGS

Abbott Laboratories, Bristol-Myers,
Sterling Drug, Warner-Lambert

of a consolidation pattern. But I hesitated because there was no confirmation from other drug stocks.

This caution paid off. Within a few months, the charts showed a gradual reversal and, by late spring, a sharp selloff with other one-time favorites.

That's the way to catch shifts in industry trends and to find new line-drive stocks. But you may have to be patient and wait for the real upmove to prove out.

10. For Maximum Profits, Choose Quality Stock

For years, the Wall Street establishment—the banks, the brokerage firms, the New York Stock Exchange and the financial media—have been preaching that you should "invest for the long term."

I believe that the small investor should ignore such counsel. If you want to make long-term profits, put your money in high-quality real estate and don't go near the stock market. Stocks are too risky to have a chunk of your savings tied up when you are not willing to pay attention to their management for relatively short-term profits.

The time to benefit from investments in securities is when the stock market is going UP. Then there's no better place to make money. Stocks are more liquid and far more rewarding than real estate or any other type of investment.

My advice holds for shares of mutual funds. The investment company hierarchy preaches that their pooled funds are ideal vehicles for long-term growth. But the record shows a catch that most people overlook: in a bear market, you'll be clobbered. Don't let anyone convince you that these pooled investment shares are either safe or profitable long-term holdings.

In a bull market you can't miss with these diversified portfolios. Buy fund shares only in an UP market: sell them going into a DOWN market. This way you can keep your capital.

I say this even though I have many friends in the investment company business and realize that if every investor followed my advice, my friends would be out of jobs in bear markets.

PICKING STOCKS

In picking stocks, I don't use astrology or shoot craps. The choice of profitable investments is hard work. You have to be informed, gain perspectives and do your homework. Every day I read *The Wall Street Journal, The New York Times* and the *New York Daily News.* On Sunday, I add *Barron's,* which is delivered to my home. And throughout the week, I study general and business magazines such as *Business Week, New York Magazine* and *Saturday Review.*

I read these publications because I realize that Wall Street does not operate in a vacuum. It is an incredibly sensitive community which is affected by what happens around the world. I pick up ideas and concepts that help me to catch trends early.

Months before President Ford's WIN program, which, as with most political panaceas, came too late, I stayed ahead of the crowd because of an article in the *Saturday Review.* At that time the great concern was double-digit inflation. But editor Norman Cousins, in his usual thoughtful style, insisted that rampant inflation had ceased to be a major threat. I agreed and changed my thinking accordingly.

OTHER SOURCES

I also check the research reports and letters being fed to institutions by large banking and brokerage houses and well-established investment-advisory firms. Their comments keep me on track with the current thinking of fundamental analysts.

I ignore all reports and analyses by the research departments of large wire houses. My experience has shown them to be completely—well, almost—useless.

With a broad informational background, I am in a better position to use the heart of my investment-decision data: the technical chart services.

Over a weekend, I spend up to six hours doing my homework and mapping strategy for the week ahead. This may seem a great deal of time but I am covering a broad field for myself and for my clients. As an individual investor, you should be able to get the information you need by concentrated study of two hours a week, or three hours every other week.

In my own reviews, I go over every one of the 750 charts in the short-term book to locate those stocks which appear to be candidates for successful trading: long in an UP market; short in a DOWN market. I pay special attention to the charts of stocks my clients own and look for new opportunities with stocks that fit my mode of operation.

To get the overall background, I check the technical indexes described earlier: trendlines of the Dow Average, of groups by industry, etc. My first emphasis is on the sell side: which stocks, as shown by charts and confirmed by group action, are potential DOWNers or are in the midst of topping out. In mid-1976, for example, the technical indicators showed that machinery manufacturers and chemicals were falling.

Next, I correlate my information with what I saw on the ticker tape during the week. This leads to general conclusions on the immediate prospects of the market, of groups and specific stocks. A good broker learns by osmosis.

I follow the same pattern with stocks I am trading or consider trading and end up by checking the three chart books: daily, intermediate-term and long-term. I update my Watch list by eliminating poor performers and adding potential winners. I double-check the fundamentals to be sure there are no new negatives such as lower earnings, new debt, etc. Finally I make the sell and buy decisions for my clients and for my own account.

TRADE FOR PROFITS

These detailed studies are especially valuable in short-term trading. If I "feel" a stock is wrong, I do not hesitate to sell a quarter of a point within a day, or even an hour, after purchase. The name of the game is *to make money*. There's no logic in losing or throwing good money after bad. I trade for profits, but when I am wrong, I take fast, small losses. My clients are trained to practice these concepts.

On March 25, 1975, I purchased for a client 400 shares of Diamond Shamrock (DIA) at 28. This was a major, high-quality chemical company whose charts indicated an UP breakthrough. In the next 11 months, DIA went through the roof to a high of 75. This was an extraordinary large, quick profit.

In late February 1976, my client suggested we liquidate the position. I disagreed and urged him to hold because the overall market was good. The stock was in an uptrend; yet I kept a close tab on the momentum.

My client was right. Four weeks later the stock was down to 71. I looked at the entire chemical group and saw indications that there could be a major correction, probably over 15 percent.

I called my client, apologized for my error, and admitted that his instinct to sell DIA was right. We agreed to get out. The chart showed a clearcut

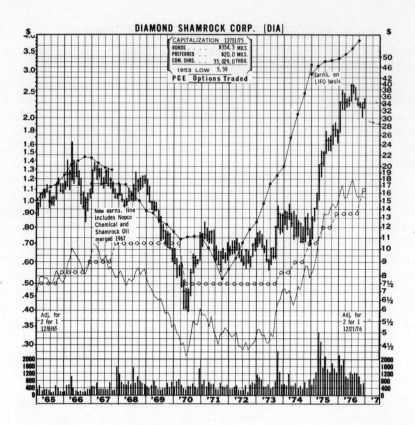

CAPITALIZATION 12/31/75
BONDS . . . . $354.3 MILS.
PREFERRED . . $20.0 MILS.
COM. SHRS. . . 33,029.0 THOU.
1953 LOW 5.39
P C E   Options Traded

Earns. on LIFO basis

New earns. line includes Nopco Chemical and Shamrock Oil merged 1967

Adj. for 2 for 1 12/8/65

Adj. for 2 for 1 12/21/76

'65 '66 '67 '68 '69 '70 '71 '72 '73 '74 '75 '76 '7

break at 71, but I was still a bit dubious so I allowed the stock to go a point or two out of the channel in hopes that it would get back to its winning ways. When the price went under 70, we sold.

My client didn't gripe that we missed selling at the top. Sensibly, he was pleased with his large, long-term capital gain. Once again, gut feeling (my client's) and technical analysis (mine) proved profitable.

The decision was confirmed by the long-term chart: the stock had not been above the 28/29 level since 1969. Earnings of the company, and the chemical industry as a whole, were in a strong uptrend when the stock was purchased on a technical breakout at 29/30. (Actually, we anticipated that signal by one point). The chart pattern was so favorable that I felt sure the stock would explode. There was confirmation along the line. In November 1975, DIA broke its 1966 high of 50—an almost sure signal of higher prices to come. In this case it was so significant that we held during the correction from 57 to 50, even though selling would have assured a substantial gain. Then came a period of consolidation followed by another line drive—to 75.

This was a time when many people might have become greedy. This is always an important factor in trading. Fortunately, my client knew that when you become hoggish, you can get burned. When DIA broke through its uptrend line, he had sufficient confidence in technical analysis and was disciplined enough to take his profit and not lament that he might have made a few more points. To experienced traders, the risks of overvaluation are greater than the potential rewards.

DETERMINING QUALITY

Institutional investors use varying criteria but always insist on quality, which, by Webster's definition, is "excellence of character . . . thoroughbred."

Generally the quality corporation, as determined by fundamental analysis, must have:

• *Adequate resources*, in current and potential assets, to continue to expand. What is "adequate" must be related to the industry. Fifty million dollars in cash and securities may be ample for a retailer but it's not enough for an international oil firm.

• *Manageable debt*, not so heavy that, in recessions, most of the income must be used to pay interest and amortization, leaving little for the common stockholders.

• *Capitalization*, large enough to permit the institutions to buy and sell substantial blocks of shares without upsetting the market. Generally this means a minimum of 5,000,000 shares of common stock owned by 2,000 stockholders.

• *Strong ownership*, as indicated by holdings of major investors: at least 300,000 shares in the hands of ten or more institutions.

An easy-to-use guideline is the ranking in Standard & Poor's Stock Guide. This is based on the corporation's ten-year record of "earnings and dividends" performance which ". . . is the end result of the interplay . . . the assessment of numerous factors such as product and industry position, the multifaceted aspects of managerial capacity, corporate financial policy and resources . . . growth and stability of earnings and dividends . . ." etc.

A+ Highest	B+ Average
A High	B Below Average
A— Above Average	B— Lower

Quality stocks are those rated A— or higher. Once in a while I will trade those rated B+ when all of the signals are Go.

The final, and most significant, criterion in institutional selection is the company's earnings growth rate: How fast have the profits increased in the past and how fast can they be expected to advance in the future?

A premium corporation is one whose annual rate of growth for the past five, and preferably ten, years has been at least 10 percent and can be expected to be sustained or bettered in the near future.

STICK WITH QUALITY

Let me repeat: Buy quality. If you time your purchases properly, your losses will be few and small and your profits will be frequent and substantial. The chances of a continued up drive will be greater than of a sudden downbreak: the pattern of movement will be fairly well defined and predictable. Unseasoned, poor-quality equities are volatile, unpredictable and seldom worthwhile. The institutions concentrate their holdings in stocks of big, dominant, financially strong, profitable, quality companies. Go thou and do likewise!

You can drop a bundle when you forget this and succumb to the lure of "hot" stocks. This is what happened in late 1968 when new issues of small companies were flooding the over-the-counter market. Many of my clients got speculation fever. They wanted to buy what I considered junk: shares of poor quality, risky, highly promoted corporations.

These men were not neophytes or losers seeking to retrieve their losses. They were smart individuals who had made a great deal of money in the long bull market. But suddenly they forgot discipline and calm, intelligent market strategy.

ONE PUTAWAY STOCK

There's only one stock that I would consider a "putaway"—one that I might hold for the duration of a bull market: International Business Machines (IBM). This is top quality and held in every institutional portfolio.

I cannot envision the market going up without a strong move by this money-making international giant. Nor can I believe that the stock market will stay strong after the IBM chart shows a downside breakout. Note how closely IBM's pattern moves with that of the Dow Jones Industrial Average.

To get back to my clients with speculation fever: They were overcome by greed and envisioned doubling their money in two months and running $20,000 to $200,000 in one year. They were not trading or even speculating. They were gambling.

Now the last thing I am is stodgy. I know from experience that any kind of stock market investment can be risky. I also know that winning investors have to be sensible, intelligent, and professional. In meeting after meeting with these clients, I stressed my ideas of quality and concentration. Both of these principles ruled out buying junk.

I repeated that I could not and would not sanction such foolish purchases just to make commissions. I pointed out that, if they bought these swingers, they shouldn't be surprised if they got insomnia and worried all night about whether they'd have any money left the next morning.

I told them the tale of one client who, through hard work and disciplined trading, built $25,000 into $100,000, then caught gambling fever. He forgot everything that had proven successful. He put all his money into six junk issues—on margin. In a few months he was completely wiped out. He lost

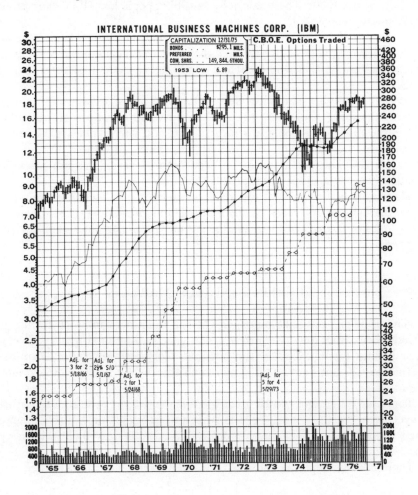

INTERNATIONAL BUSINESS MACHINES CORP. (IBM)

all his profits plus his principal. Halfway through the story, my clients weren't listening.

Finally, after all my arguments had failed, I explained that, as far as I was concerned, they had four choices:

1. To forget this insanity and go back to the proven-profitable trading techniques

2. To withdraw 25 percent of their account and trade it with another broker

3. To close out their entire account with me and find another broker

4. To give me their orders to be processed without advice or comment

Unfortunately, four of the ten clients chose option 3. The results were disastrous. The new selections looked like the uranium stocks that were the hotshots of the 1950s. These normally sensible people lost all of their profits and dented their capital.

A year or so later, some of the losers saved me from saying "I told you so." They called me to ask if I would take their accounts again, because "You are one of the few brokers who preached good-quality stocks and stuck to your guns."

Such catastrophic gambling sprees are typical of every bull market. Usually the fever comes near the market top when all values are distorted. When the break does come, it's fast, furious and very expensive as can be clearly seen by the chart of Fairchild Camera & Instrument Corporation (Chapter 4). The declines can be even more devastating with stocks of small, unseasoned companies traded OTC.

These ten clients were not unique. The same greed affected thousands of stock market traders, most of them small, individual investors. Since the stock market is cyclical, you can bet your last dollar this stupidity will happen again.

FREEBEES IN BULL MARKETS

With apologies to the able people who run the American Stock Exchange, I trade their issues only when they are of good institutional quality. Few of their listings qualify. Two of the possible selections are Syntex Corp. and Carnation Co. But here again, I buy such stocks only when they are moving UP.

The same caveat goes, with greater emphasis, for over-the-counter issues. Never bother with "young, aggressive future Polaroids or Xeroxes." Leave such speculations to the hardy souls who have crystal balls that never shatter.

There is one exception: hot new issues in a strong bull market when they are available at genuine bargain prices. If you are one of the few people who generate over $10,000 a year commission business, press your broker to give you a "freebee." These are shares of a new issue for which the brokerage firm is the underwriter. They are worthwhile speculations because they are almost guaranteed to rise.

Example: The stock is priced at $15 a share but is so popular that it will open at $23 for an $8 instant profit. Take your gain and run. Such fast moves do happen on Wall Street. Someone gets these bargains. So why not you?

DON'T NEGLECT GLAMOUR STOCKS

Some people are leery of glamour stocks: shares of famous-name companies such as Avon, Disney, Eastman Kodak and Texas Instruments. They say, "These may be great stocks but they cost too much, are too volatile and too risky for my portfolio."

Don't believe it. Institutional money managers know that this is not true. They consider these glamour stocks less expensive, less volatile and less risky than lower-quality issues. The people who are afraid of the glamours don't think clearly or do their homework. They become paranoid when they hear a radio commentator say, "The Dow Jones Industrial Average was down eight points. It was a bad day on Wall Street. The glamours were hit hard: Texas Instruments, at 124, down 1⅛; Eastman Kodak, at 100, down ¾; IBM, at 250, down 2½; and Dow Chemical, at 92, off a point."

These doleful reports sound big and important. But do your own figuring to see why such small losses are not significant. If you have 200 shares of Dow ($18,400) and it drops one point, you lose $200.

On the other hand, if you have 500 shares of Whiz-Bang Electronics at 10 ($5,000) and it drops ⅜, the $187.50 dollar loss is about the same, but the percentage drop is three times as great as that of the glamour.

Most important, as you'll learn by experience, the big, active institutional stocks, traveling in the right direction, are much less susceptible to major market dips.

THE IMPORTANCE OF LIQUIDITY

Another strong reason for trading active stocks is liquidity. You can get in and out quickly—it's easier to buy or sell 100 or 1,000 shares within an eighth of a point. These institutional favorites have large capitalizations so that the professional money manager can trade 25,000 shares without disturbing the market too much.

There may be only a small price change, but any trade of this size, even when made over a couple of days, will show up immediately on the chart and the tape. The heavier volume will alert me and other technical analysts that something is happening and this may be the time to jump aboard.

With the "herd instinct," trading will increase, and with it the price of the stock. Now you have a line-drive stock. You should be in the middle of this move, watching your profits climb.

IMPORTANCE OF PAST PERFORMANCE

Plan your trading strategy against what has happened to the stock before—clearly evident on the long-term chart. In June 1976, I noticed that Minnesota Mining & Manufacturing Co. (MMM) was forming a channel and, despite the generally slow market, was moving up. Checking the chart, I saw that its trend could push up to 70, above the 1975 high.

This was a quality stock and had recently been added to the components of the Dow Jones Industrial Average. The group was acting well and the market was generally moving UP. I started buying.

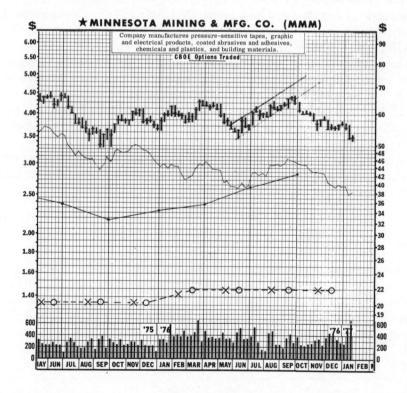

I looked for resistance at 65, which had been its high in March, but I felt that it could still go higher, possibly to 70, the top of its channel. Under the rules of technical analysis, this would be the peak because: (1) it would occur within a little more than a year after the previous high in 1975; (2) the interim high would be below the 1973 record of 91. I sold at 65 for a 15-point profit.

Past performance is a sound, logical basis for setting sell targets. The professionals are watching those charts, too.

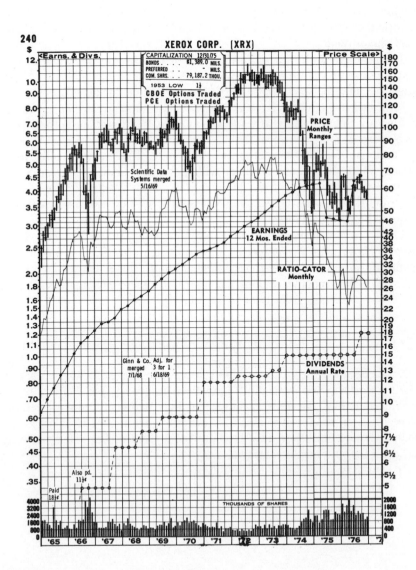

SKIP DOWN STOCKS

In all investing, it is important to determine whether the quality issue you are considering is an UP or a DOWN stock. Some brokers, and many clients, believe in trading DOWN. They know that once a stock has established a definite downtrend there is usually a market correction with a sizable rebound.

This happened with Xerox in 1965 when the stock fell from over 90 to below 50 in a few months, then bounced back to over 100. Later, this same up-and-down pattern was repeated with relatively small price swings. Such situations seldom offer the 20 percent gain potential which is the goal of every investment.

The problem with buying DOWN stocks is the decision on when to sell. If you guess right and there is a rebound, there's no problem. But what if you are wrong and the stock continues to decline? When do you sell?

Let's say you bought Xerox at 75 on its way down from 90. You hope it will go up. But will you still want to own it at 45? If you made the purchase on 50 percent margin, you're about wiped out.

You must consider what other investors may do. If there's a rally, even of two or three points, more sellers will move in and bang the price down again. Institutions with losses are likely to go on a selling spree and start dumping their shares. Once again, the supply will exceed the demand, and you will be holding a loser.

There are brokers who specialize in buying DOWN stocks. They are *bargain hunters*. If your broker suggests you adopt such a tactic, question his judgment. If he continues such recommendations, think about shifting your account. These people seldom change. With their clients, they form the largest segment of regular losers, year after year.

ONE FINAL WARNING

Never fight the institutions. One reason why you can make money with quality stocks is that institutions have become predictable. When they start buying or selling, the odds are high that they will continue such action for some time: on the UP side until they have a profit of at least 20 percent; on the DOWN side until they have sold out their position. Use these patterns of behavior for your own advantage.

In summary, always look for quality stocks that are:

1. Technically and fundamentally good. If there's conflict between the two analyses, go with the chart signals

2. UP stocks
3. In an UP group
4. In an UP market
5. Rated B+ or better
6. Owned by at least 10 large shareholders
7. In the top tier (the first 5 companies) of a group
8. Actively traded

Hard work keeps me razor-sharp and makes money for me. It can do the same for you. Success requires time and discipline. But I have many accounts; you have only one. If you are truly dedicated to making profits in the stock market, you'll find time to develop the knowledge and discipline to follow the Blackman Strategy and make money for yourself.

By confining your selections to quality stocks, you will improve your reward/risk ratio. The chances of gains are surer and the likelihood of losses less than if you fool around with secondary, speculative issues that are seldom candidates for institutional portfolios.

11.   The Fine Art of Selling

Selling is a fine art. It's the one area where few investors, large or small, professional or amateur, do well. Yet wise selling is essential to maximum profits in the stock market. This requires strict attention to technical analysis, adherence to basic rules, and a sense of timing. I've made a successful living and have built a profitable business by learning how and when to sell.

In reading books about the stock market, I have found the same three theories of so-called successful selling repeated: *Always sell:*

1. When you see trouble coming to the industry in which you own stock

2. When you see another security that is better for you to own

3. In a bear market. Then sell some shares and, as the market continues down, keep selling—weak stocks first. But hold your strong stocks

To my mind, not one of these "rules" is worth following. They don't make sense, nor do they work. Here's why:

1. *Industry trouble.* No one can predict accurately what will happen in the next six months or a year. I mean no one in the financial/investment area: not the Secretary of the Treasury, not the head of the Federal Reserve Board, not the wisest economist, and certainly not me or you. In today's wide world, there are too many powerful forces that can change conditions almost overnight. Remember the oil crisis? When everything concerned with oil was supposed to be in deep trouble? The panic was severe but short-lived.

As a theory, the idea of selling stocks because an industry *may* get into trouble sounds great, but it is usually meaningless. You cannot foresee the future well enough to justify a sale for that one reason.

Once in a while you can piece together bits of information that will give you warning that it's time to sell. But this is the exception, not the rule. This

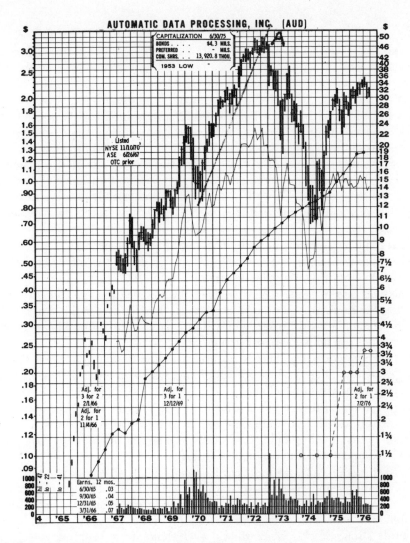

AUTOMATIC DATA PROCESSING, INC. (AUD)

CAPITALIZATION 6/30/75
BONDS . . . . $4.3 MILS.
PREFERRED . . - MILS.
COM. SHRS. . . 13,920.8 THOU.

1953 LOW

Listed
NYSE 11/10/70
ASE 6/26/67
OTC prior

Adj. for
3 for 2
2/1/66

Adj. for
2 for 1
11/4/66

Adj. for
3 for 1
12/12/69

Adj. for
2 for 1
7/2/76

Earns. 12 mos.
6/30/65   .03
9/30/65   .04
12/31/65   .05
3/31/66   .07

happened with Automatic Data Processing (AUD) in early 1973. AUD was one of the miracle stocks between 1965 and 1972. It rose from 2 to 100.

AUD's basic business was preparing data-processing services for Wall Street brokerage firms. Back offices relied on its service, and for a long time AUD was one of the favorites for both their institutional and personal portfolios.

In late February 1973, a new client came into our office. At the first conference, the key question was: Should he sell his large block (over 10,000 shares) of AUD at about 75? He had a whopping profit, as he had bought at an adjusted price of about 5.

I explained why I believed that AUD was no longer an UP stock: that, in the last quarter, it had broken its long-term uptrend line. Once it hit the 100 mark, it had dropped to give a clear sell signal.

This explanation did not hit the new client's sell button.

Then, I told him that: (a) The owners of several brokerage firms had this stock as one of their core positions in their own portfolios and some were starting to sell. He still was not convinced; (b) That Wall Street was going through a period of recession that rivaled the bleak 1930s and I believed that half the firms would close or be merged. Still no decision; (c) Several of these firms used AUD in their back office, and friends of mine in those organizations had told me that they were considering selling their personal holdings.

That did it. My new client said, "That makes sense to me. Sell."

The stock went at an average price of over 70. Later the same year, AUD dropped to around 38. By 1974, it was down below 22.

This was one instance where *knowing* in advance that an industry was heading for trouble helped make a wise sell decision. Over the years, with experience and a good broker, you will find similar situations where "inside information" can help you to sell at a profit.

2. *Better opportunity.* This is sensible but doesn't tell you when to sell your present holdings. It does not aid timing, which, in my experience, is the most important aspect of selling.

This is a logical theory but is difficult to put into practice. You may have good reason to sell, but there's no way to be sure that the new stock will perform better. A sale should stand on its own merits, not on hope that some other investment will prove more rewarding.

3. *Bear market.* As with most pat formulas, this is always dangerous, and usually bunk. When you believe that everything points to a down market, that means there will be continuing declines in stock prices. Rather than dribble out your shares at ever increasing losses, liquidate your entire account: strong stocks, weak stocks, everything. In a bear market, *good* stocks soon become *bad* stocks. Stop kidding yourself. Become completely liquid and put your money in a savings account until there's an upturn. Or, if conditions justify, sell short.

ART OF TIMING

None of these theories mention what I believe is the most important ingredient of successful selling: *the art of timing.*

Trading in the stock market is like music. A musician is lost without a sense of timing. Either he's born with it or he has to learn it. No matter how it's acquired, a sense of timing is essential to good music. If you look at the stock market as a symphony, full of complex rhythms and changing melodies, to play it successfully requires a sense of timing that is as acute as a musician's. *And the key to that timing is technical analysis.*

In the past 16 years, I've been a successful trader 80 percent of the time. But when I fell in love with a stock, disregarded the charts and did not sell, I became an involuntary investor (one who buys for a quick profit but ends up by holding the stock with a loss). In such a situation, I almost always lost money on these rule-breakers. I've learned my lesson the hard way.

THE FAILURE OF FUNDAMENTAL ANALYSIS

With fundamental analysis, there is no way to know when to sell a stock. This may sound blunt, but it is true. When you hold a stock entirely on the strength of its basic value, you become subjective. Selling by technical analysis forces you to be objective. You act on the action shown by the charts, and as you will learn, charts don't lie.

Let me explain why I am so convinced that fundamental analysis is not effective in timing selling. Basically, most fundamental analysts are statisticians. They base their recommendations on future projections, not on what is actually happening in the market place. In the long run their evaluations may be correct, but realization may take years. In that period, the smart trader has made half a dozen profitable deals. He may have taken a few fast, small losses, but he has also achieved several large, relatively quick profits.

To prove my point, let's follow the typical security analyst. After studying the past records of a corporation, he visits the company for a few hours or days and comes back an industry expert.

At the plant he'll talk to various division heads, production managers and even the sweeper to gauge corporate morale. Then he'll walk into the treasurer's office and ask, "What's your estimate of earnings for the fourth quarter and for the next year?"

The analyst may or may not get a direct answer, but, by quoting predictions of other researchers, he'll go away with a figure. This will be included in a 90-page, in-depth report, which will be distributed to institutional clients. Like parrots, other Wall Street analysts and institutional money managers will quote that magic estimate. It will become gospel, yet in most cases will not be accurate.

Most corporate executives try to be factual, but since they want their company's stock to go up, they tend to be biased. Often they use poor judgment, either understating or overstating what they feel are the company's current earnings and potential.

In my experience, management's estimates of profits are usually meaningless. The analyst should make his own projections, just as he uses his own judgment in preparing the research report.

The only time I fully trust corporate management is when I've read reports that "insiders" have been buying or selling company stock. I like the idea that the president has just bought stock in the open market or that a director has doubled his position from 15,000 to 30,000 shares. And usually I like to see a new president who comes into a company with a big stock option. I know that he'll work like the devil to make sure that the option can be exercised for substantial profits.

I'll admit that there are some corporations which over the years have built reputations for honesty in their information to analysts and the financial press. But these companies are rare, and usually are large organizations with skilled experienced officers and directors.

Frankly, I'm skeptical of almost everything that executives of smaller companies tell me. Here's one example:

A few years ago, my firm issued a bullish report on Jewelcor, Inc., a jewelry catalogue company. The stock went up to $30 a share when management announced that there would be a new stock offering to raise capital needed to finance the expanding sales. Our analyst was assured that everything looked great, that current earnings were good and future prospects better.

But our research director was not satisfied. He discovered that part of the secondary issue would include shares being sold by the president and several key executives for "tax benefits, diversification of assets, etc." This raised the red flag.

We halted all purchase recommendations, and when the stock turned technically weak, we urged selling. Based strictly on technical, not fundamental, analysis, we were right. The stock bottomed out at 2⅜.

"Insider" information can be valuable. Reports of these special purchases and sales are carried in the financial press, but if you want more complete data, subscribe to a service that reports all public trades, or better yet, ask your broker to keep you current.

WHEN YOU SELL, SELL OUT

I strongly advocate selling in total, not in steps. In your decision to sell you are either right or wrong. There's no halfway position that can be profitable. Liquidate your entire position and take your gains or losses.

Selling by steps makes no sense. If the stock keeps going down, you lose more money. If it goes up, your gains will be less. And if you do not pay close attention, you may get caught by a sudden reversal. Obey the chart signals and take your profits.

Selling is one time that the individual has an advantage over the institution. No major investor can get out of a major position quickly. With thousands of shares, the professional has to sell in steps, and often gets trapped. With your modest holdings, you can sell out in no time. Here's an example:

You have 500 shares of Wonderful, Inc. The company has a capitalization of 12 million shares, of which about 25 percent are held by institutions. The average daily trading volume of the stock is between 40,000 and 50,000 shares. The stock has moved up well and is now in a consolidation pattern just above 40.

The downbreak comes at 40 soon after noon. You see this and know that the institutional technicians are watching, too. Generally you have 15 minutes to two hours to get out free because the professionals will want to "see how the stock closes."

Your broker monitors the tape and, unless there is a sharp reversal, will get you out before day's end.

The odds are that the stock will continue to drop for the next few days. If you are still hesitating about selling in hopes of a bounce back, *don't*. You'll get more today than you'll get tomorrow. With a declining stock, today's low is tomorrow's high.

Since the institutions act like cattle, that break will start a stampede. Institution A, with 90,000 shares, will want to sell at least 50,000 shares, probably 75,000, and possibly 90,000, as soon as possible. The money manager will instruct the executing broker, "Listen, we know WON only traded 40,000 shares a day. Work the orders; do the best you can; piece the sale out over a few days."

The Big Boys do not have liquidity in such situations. Since you're not part of the herd, you can take advantage of this opportunity and act on your own strength.

RULES FOR SELLING

One of the essentials of Blackman Strategy is to obey these rules. *Always sell* if only *one* of these factors is negative. The record shows that such action will be wise—and profitable—80 percent of the time.

1. *When there's a violation of the uptrend line of the stock or of the uptrend line of the Dow Jones Industrial Average* (or any other standard stock market indicator).

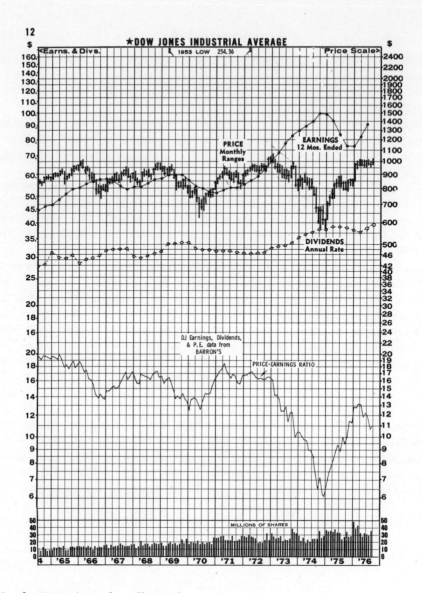

★DOW JONES INDUSTRIAL AVERAGE

<Earns. & Divs. 1953 LOW 254.36 Price Scale>

PRICE
Monthly
Ranges

EARNINGS
12 Mos. Ended

DIVIDENDS
Annual Rate

DJ Earnings, Dividends,
& P.E. data from
BARRON'S

PRICE-EARNINGS RATIO

MILLIONS OF SHARES

'65 '66 '67 '68 '69 '70 '71 '72 '73 '74 '75 '76

On the Dow chart, the sell signal came during the weeks of:
- January 30 when the average fell below 960
- April 2 when the average dropped below 992

On the Trendline chart, the Point A's signal the violation:
- in 1974: March, June, August and November
- in 1975: March and July
- in 1976: April

If you think this means a lot of activity, you're right. But it also means that investors who obeyed such signals saved themselves very substantial losses.

2. *When the stock reaches the top of the channel.*

With Teledyne, Inc., this came, after a long up drive, at 80. Note that beautiful year-long UP channel, and how the stock swung between 42 and 80, with an all-time new high at 55. What a great chance this was for trading profits!

3. *When the stock's volume reaches a six-month high.*

See the Ramada Inns, Inc., chart. In February 1976, the volume soared for two weeks. The first boom boosted the stock to a new high of 6⅝. The second big (though smaller) week was followed by an almost steady price decline to 4.

Usually, when volume reaches a record level, it's the sign of a peak price. I don't care if I miss the top by half a point or so. In fact, I hope I do so because the person who buys my stock will have an immediate paper gain. Otherwise he sinks into a loss position. At this point, he's going to stop taking my stock. Besides, it's always easier to sell an UP stock than to unload a declining one. Let the buyer profit, too.

4. *After a big hit.*

Let's assume that you have an account with $30,000 market value: $15,000 equity and 50 percent margin. You have two 1,000-share positions, both

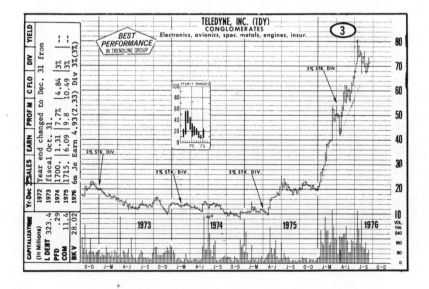

bought at 15. One stock takes a substantial move to over 20, then drops back. You sell for an after-commission profit of about $5,000.

Now you have $20,000 equity and have increased your capital by one-third. Unless the other stock is acting well and shows a strong upmove, liquidate immediately. The odds are that nothing will happen, so you're better off in cash.

This may be a time to be wary. Your broker may try to push a "switch trade"—to persuade you to sell, and to buy a new stock. After all, he's trained to "get the other side of every trade" as quickly as possible. Don't be sucked in. Take your time. Clear your head. Let the market go for three days or a week. Then make sure that the next stock you buy is the best one that you can find. When you own a stock, it's natural to become subjective. In a liquid position, you are objective, and thus can be selective.

5. *After three straight losses.*

When this sad situation occurs (and it will, inevitably, though, let us hope, not frequently), sell everything. If you sustain three losses in a row,

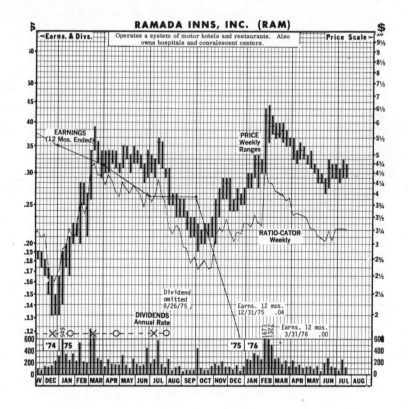

it's not you who's to blame—if you have been playing by the rules. You're in a bad market and should recognize it. Go into cash until you are reoriented and the market starts to move up again.

6. *After nine (12) months if you're fully invested.*

When I first wrote this, the original rule was "After six months." The rule was based on historical stock market action: that, over many years, the movement from a bottom to a top covered about six months—the time needed to qualify profits for the lower capital-gains tax rate. At this point, the market and upmoving stocks are likely to pause under the pressure of sales by profit-taking investors. They take control, and for a while virtually stop the market from going up.

Under the new tax law, the time period for long-term capital gains has been extended to nine months in 1977 and 12 months thereafter. But the sell rule holds because, by selling promptly at the hiatus that always occurs at the end of the holding period, you can keep your gains and avoid taking losses during the subsequent decline.

When you judge the time span, do so from the week the UPTREND started—not from the date you bought the stock. Check the charts and make believe that you bought at the bottom. Then mark your investment calendar nine months or one year from that time.

Suppose the stock went from 20 to 30 in the tax-time span. You bought in at 23. Base your projections on the day the stock first broke above 20. Then try to figure out what the institutions will do: Will they hold if there is still a strong uptrend? Will they take their profits if there's a consolidation area? In my experience, if this type of pause continues at set intervals in the future, it's wise to sell. Take your profits and wait for the start of another up drive.

This is a tough rule for most investors to accept. It should be used flexibly, but it's backed by common sense and proven profitable results. I have found it one of the few rules that works almost every time.

One thing about this rule is that obeying it makes it easy to reach the decision to liquidate. This happened with my Laboratory Account (Chapter 20). In mid-January 1975, the DJIA took off in a breakaway run. Six months later, almost to the day, the market topped out at 889. Nonbelievers will call this coincidence, more probably, dumb luck. As far as I am concerned, I sold at a good profit because I followed Rule Number 6.

This time-span concept also applies (but less frequently) to individual stocks that have had a strong rise. In the last 20 years there have been hundreds of examples of stocks soaring for six months, then pausing, consolidating, dipping and then readying for another move, either UP or DOWN. By selling, you keep your gains and are in a sound position to select the best stocks for the new rise. Even if you go back to the same issues, you will be ahead of the game.

In a way, this rule keeps you from being greedy. It retains your capital and makes you pay close attention to what's happening to the overall market and to your specific holdings.

7. *When you do not have a clear-head concept of what's happening to the stock market and to your holdings.* (This is a variation of the 6–9–12-months rule.)

Your perspective must be objective. I feel that every account, large or small, should be liquidated two or three times a year. Periodically it is wise to hold cash, clear your head, review your assets and objectives and do some hard, realistic thinking.

The best time to do this is when your account is static. You may not be losing, but you are not making money. Liquidate your stocks, wait a week, even a month, to get that clear perspective; then move into the market again *if it is moving* UP.

8. *When you become smug and cocky.*

Always sell when you find yourself saying "I'm a genius. I can do no wrong. I just had ten winners in a row."

This is the time to be wary. No one in Wall Street is a hotshot for long. It's a tough arena where every investor competes with some of the smartest (and most ruthless) people in the world. Check your own roof before it falls in. Be realistic. Don't become your own worst enemy and let overconfidence lead you into costly mistakes. *He who keeps his capital intact comes back to buy another day.*

9. *When there are no stocks to buy.*

This is a good time to sell. The market is going nowhere, so why tie up your capital and risk a sudden loss?

In September 1976 the Wall Street word was to buy and get in at the beginning of a pre-election rally. But I could not find a single strong line-drive stock. I concluded that, as usual, the "experts" were wrong and that the market would not go up. I liquidated my holdings by selling into strength during the week the market went up 37 points.

Once again, technical analysis was right. The Dow broke at 1,020, fell quickly to 935 and took a lot of my colleagues (but not my clients) to the cleaners.

10. *When there's a general technical sell signal on the market itself.*

In such a situation I sell everything—the good and the bad. If the market looks really bearish, I start selling short. In the past few years, with the widely fluctuating market, I have been in cash frequently. A good example came in 1974 when the Dow Jones Industrial Average broke at about 800. At 790 it shattered a double bottom (the two low points at the end of 1973). There was a short upmove, so my clients still had time to get out before the market took a precipitous ride down to 690.

Then came a small reverse. There was no confirmation, and the market finally went down further: to 570. By heeding the first technical signal and not flip-flopping around with baseless hopes, smart investors avoided the damage of the second 100-point drop.

SELL SIGNALS USED BY TECHNICAL ANALYSIS

No sell signal is infallible, especially when it relates to the action of the overall stock market. But as I have pointed out, the charts are accurate 80 percent of the time. There are, however, other sell signals used by technical analysts. I do not agree fully with all of them but they are worth mentioning to point out how complex some analysts can make a simple subject. I believe charts are more graphic, more accurate and easier to understand than these other sell signals.

Most technicians feel that when one third of the following situations exist, it's a warning signal. When the number rises to more than half, sell promptly. All of these conditions relate to selling. Since some are more important than others, I've starred* these for ready reference.

Rampant bullishness from Wall Street to Main Street. Everyone, even the least clever and inexperienced, is making money in the stock market. Nobody thinks of selling. The only word is to buy, more and more. Pundits talk of a "New Era" of investment, and even young secretaries are boasting of their capital gains.

Repeated nonconfirmations by the Dow Jones Industrial and Transportation Averages, even though one or the other may make a new high. (*Note:* One of the basic tenets of the Dow Theory of stock market action is that a bull market is signaled only when both the Industrial and Transportation Averages break into new highs.)

Very heavy trading volume with little or no advance in the major market averages (Dow Jones Industrials, NYSE Composite and S&P's 500 Stock Price Index).

New highs in the Dow Jones Industrial Average but a lack of confirmation from the Advance/Decline Line.

This is a significant divergence because it shows that although some Dow stocks may still be going up, the majority of issues are going nowhere. Check the charts.

Repeated new highs in the market averages with more new lows for individual stocks.

This is most effective when the Dow Industrials keep moving up but shares of other major corporations decline.

*A *pattern of declining volume on rallies and increasing volume on declines.*

The market is running out of steam; investors are becoming cautious; more people are reluctant to buy and anxious to sell.

* *Broad weakness in the bond market: yields on new debt offerings rising rapidly.*

Higher interest rates affect bonds and stocks similarly—i.e., they depress prices.

*Three *increases in the discount rate as set by the Federal Reserve Board, within three to six months.*

When these raises total more than two percentage points, credit is tightening. That's always a bad sign for the future of stock prices.

Persistent and rapid runups in the prices of commodities.

You can watch these changes in the financial press—the news stories and the daily quotations for such major commodities as wheat, corn, soybeans, coffee, pork bellies, etc. When prices of these essential ingredients of food and industrial products keep rising, it's a sure sign of trouble ahead. Soon manufacturing and processors will have to boost the prices of their products, and living costs will jump and corporate profits will be squeezed. In 1973–74, the higher prices of copper, sugar and grains rose rapidly, forecasting the 1975 drop in the stock market.

*The *200-day moving average flattens out and the most recent averages make penetrations of the chart line with increasing volume.*

With a moving average, the most recent figure is added and the oldest data are deleted. Since new additions will be higher than those dropped, the average will move up. When it shifts too far and too fast, the stock market is getting out of hand. Soon there's bound to be a reaction, and down go prices.

The 200-day moving average of leading stocks such as GM, IBM and AT&T follows the same pattern as described above.

Be especially wary when this lack of upward movement is accompanied by failures to make new highs with heavy volume.

More top stocks on the "new low" list.

When you see the names of blue chips on this daily tabulation, it's a sure sign that major investors are selling their positions and retreating to cash or other investments. Up momentum has ceased and a reversal is occurring.

In the fall of 1976, cyclical stocks, such as those of steels and machinery manufacturers, started to decline just before the sharp market break.

The appearance on charts of distribution tops: double tops, triple tops, head and shoulders, etc.

When these patterns begin to appear on the charts of leading stocks and/or market averages, they indicate that the steam is gone and big investors are no longer buying heavily.

More declining stocks on the Most Active list.

This is always a sign for review, and when the daily decliners include institutional favorites, this shows that investor sentiment is becoming bearish.

Increase in the number of stock splits and secondary offerings.

When corporations start to increase the shares of outstanding stock, their directors feel that the stock market is buoyant and nearing a high level. A rise in the number of secondary issues indicates that many large shareholders want to become more liquid.

Light short selling by odd-lotters.

The signal point usually is when the monthly report shows that the ratio of short sales to total sales (of all NYSE stocks) is less than $4/10$ of 1%. Ask your broker about this.

Heavy public speculation as indicated by:
1. Active trading of low-priced stocks listed on the AMEX or sold OTC
2. Increase in the buying of call options
3. A rapid advance in the S&P Low-Priced Stock Index, followed by a collapse of these marginal equities

This is a good early warning signal. The last stocks to run in a "toppy" market are the low-priced "cats and dogs." These are also the first stocks to be unloaded when there are signs of trouble ahead.

SUMMARY

The rules in this chapter may be confusing, technical and far from what you have been taught to believe. But they are logical, and they are the same rules that institutional money managers rely on.

If you still have questions, discuss my ideas with your RR. He may not fully understand (and probably won't agree with) all of these rules but his firm should have a technical analyst who can be helpful. If he/she is a skilled practitioner, you can get extra help from the daily indexes compiled to show a general technical sell signal on the market. Here's one case where a little knowledge, on your part, is not dangerous but quite beneficial.

Under all conditions, regardless of what's happening in Wall Street, sell out when you stop making money. Put the proceeds in the bank, stand on the sidelines and watch the market go by . . . and start declining.

Remember: You put your money into stocks not to break even, not to make the equivalent of bank interest, and certainly not to compete with your friends and neighbors. You invested your money to make it grow.

If this is not happening, liquidate your account, regardless of what your broker tells you. And don't go back until the time is right: when you can find UP stocks in UP groups in an UP market.

If you have gotten to the point where you want only safety and certainty, invest for fixed income: in a savings account or AAA bonds. At the current interest rates of 8 to 9 percent, those bonds will double your money in eight to nine years. If you don't feel you can better these returns in the stock market, sell and stay out. If any investor wants to hold stocks for several years, he should be so wealthy that he can afford to be wrong. I'm not that rich, and I doubt that most of you readers are, either. The only way to make real profits with stocks is to trade: to buy on the UPtrend and to sell when there's a downside break. That's all that these rules indicate.

CAVEAT

There is no surefire system to stock market success. But the Blackman Strategy is one approach that works most of the time. It's important to buy wisely, but it's a lot more important to know how and when to sell. If you follow the rules and guidelines here, you will probably be considered a "selling genius" by your friends and your broker. This will boost your ego and retain your original capital and most, or all, of your profits. Unfortunately, nine out of ten investors fail to do this.

No matter how ebullient the market, you won't make money every month.

On a yearly basis, you should be in a cash position about 20 percent of the time.

Most brokers will discourage this logical approach. They fear that you'll leave them and the market, or go to a new broker. That's why the average RR tries to keep his clients fully invested.

My advice in such circumstances: If your present broker disagrees strongly with this approach—leave him. It's like a bad marriage; it will only get worse. A broker who insists that every account be fully invested, regardless of market climate or stock performance, is not doing his job. Avoid these "switch brokers" at all costs and at all times.

In the next chapter you'll learn why it pays to be a good seller.

12. How to Be a Successful Seller

BE WILLING TO TAKE THE FAST, SMALL LOSS

I like to play seven-card stud poker but I do not enjoy gambling. It's the same with the stock market. When I'm playing stud, if I can't beat the table with my first three or four cards, I cut my losses and sit out the hand. I'll do this until I draw cards that give me a good chance to win.

This seems like a simple, logical, easy-to-follow rule; but too many players forget the odds and stay in the game because they feel they will be lucky— their last three cards will all be aces. Or they think, If I can fill that inside straight, I'll make a killing. But the odds are against them.

I believe in playing only when the odds are in my favor. If I can sit for an hour losing antes and opening bets and not getting suckered into a hand that can't win, chances are that I'm due for good cards. Such discipline is hard on my ego (and the other players' patience), but it's essential if I hope to walk away with some kind of profit.

The major point of this chapter is that you must be willing to take a fast, small loss in order to keep your capital intact and be ready for the Big Hit. This seems like a simple rule to follow, but in reality it's one of the most difficult decisions in investing. It requires discipline, which is never easy for anyone, even when it involves hard-earned savings.

A disciplined stock market trader, like a disciplined poker player, will often be successful. He learns to take the small loss, and when he has a winner, he concentrates his capital to take in enough to cover his losses. If you can't do this, you haven't really won a thing!

This same concentration principle applies to investing in the stock market. In trading stocks you should have at least seven winners in every ten transactions. This is the point where my analogy with poker playing has to be set aside. In card games you may be able to lose frequently and come back with one or two big hands, but in the stock market you can't afford to lose in more than three out of every ten deals.

By taking those quick, small losses, you'll have less anguish than if you're losing regularly, and there will be no temptation to gamble. Too many people who play the stock market rely on luck to carry them through. They have lots of luck—and it's all bad.

It's easy to lose money in the stock market when you fail to set rules and to discipline yourself to obey them. You can lose voluntarily and involuntarily.

If you decide not to sell because "the stock is experiencing a normal technical correction" and it goes down and stays down, you have a voluntary loss.

If you decide to keep the stock "until I can get even or have a smaller loss," you have become an involuntary investor. You're stuck with the stock, probably for a long time.

FORGET ABOUT TAXES

What about your tax position? Unless you are in the 50 percent tax bracket, forget it. For most investors, Uncle Sam pays the short-term losses because they are largely deductible against ordinary income, and long-term gains are taxed at only half the regular rate. The overwhelming consideration should always be the investment, not the tax effect.

Think of taxes this way: If you are making $30,000 a year and your employer offers you a $10,000 raise, you wouldn't refuse it because the added money would be taxed as ordinary income!

In stocks, losses can be made up with short-term trading. With new clients who come to our firm after they've had heavy losses, we have made up the deficit in 12 to 18 months. One executive who had taken a $42,000 shellacking told me, "To hell with taxes. I'll pay them. Let's start trading and get some profits."

Another client who learned the hard way was a recently retired gentleman. He was a boardroom sitter who spent his days watching the tape. In the spring of 1976, he told me, "Dick, I've been investing for nearly forty years and have never done really well in the market. I've been here long enough to hear you advising clients to take small, fast losses. You admit your mistakes quickly and have made out well, for yourself and your clients."

I was concerned that he was not making as much as we both agreed he should, especially in the strong UP market. He explained that his inability to

accept losses was the one factor that had prevented him from being successful in the stock market. For 40 years he had been trying to fill an inside
straight. I told him that he would be successful if he could change his
approach and exercise the discipline to sell securities in which he had little
faith because they were not performing well.

He followed my advice and in a few months discovered one of the keys to
success in the stock market. He made money—more than at any time in his
financial career.

If you get one idea from this book, let this be it: Regardless of when or
how much stock you bought, if the stock goes down, sell promptly and take
your loss. When a stock breaks its uptrend line, sell. You will be right nine
out of ten times. You will never be caught in that agonizing dilemma: Is my
stock having a normal correction or is it finished?

Or, in my language, Is it becoming a DOWN stock? *The most common
mistake of all investors, large and small, is not selling a stock for a small
loss.*

GUIDELINES

I don't know of any successful formula to determine what percentage you
should let a stock drop before selling it. It depends on the size of your
account, your temperament and the action of the stock. Here are some
guidelines which may be helpful but should be used flexibly:

As a rule of thumb, do not hold a stock when it falls 8 percent below the
price you paid. If you should miss this, never hold when the drop is as much
as 15 percent.

I learned the value of this 15 percent figure from one of my clients. As a
businessman, he realized the importance of limiting his losses. From years of
experience, he determined that the maximum loss he could afford was 15
percent. This makes sense.

When you are trading on margin, cut that loss limit to 5 percent. You are
working on borrowed capital.

Personally, I try to restrict my losses to 3 to 5 percent of my capital. I do
this even though I have to sell a day or two after purchase. Sometimes I do
not wait for a chart signal. If I feel uncomfortable, I sell.

Example: A stock, bought at 30, should *probably* be sold if it drops to
28¾ or 28½; *certainly* when it hits the 27¾ to 27½ range.

DISCRETIONARY ACCOUNT

If you set up a discretionary account by turning the management of your money over to a bank, broker or investment adviser for a fee, follow these guidelines:

• Give only limited power of attorney. This restricts the decisions to buying and selling and does not permit withdrawal of any money;

• Order immediate liquidation when there's a loss of 15 percent of your capital. Say this and mean it. The final words on Wall Street are always, Did I make or lose money? And how much?

If your account has depreciated by 15 percent, the market was bad, the money manager was incompetent or it's a combination of both. Do not care what the reason; try to preserve the remaining 85 percent of your capital.

Don't be naïve about such drastic orders. Your broker/adviser will try to talk you out of such restrictions, but you must be disciplined and, like the true professional, cut your losses immediately.

If you still have the urge to buy stocks, wait a few weeks. Use that time to clear your head and study the market. Then, make a thorough search for a new broker or money manager.

Note: This 15 percent loss limit applies to mutual funds, too. It's financial suicide to hold such shares in a bear market. There's truth in the Wall Street truism, "In bear markets, money returns to its rightful owners [the short sellers]." Take your money back and let the other fellow be the long-term investor.

SELLING IS TOUGH

Buying is easy. Selling is tough. If the stock goes down, you were wrong. Admit it and get out quickly with that fast, small loss. Otherwise you will deplete your assets.

This is such a logical premise; why do some investors refuse to believe it? And why do so many people who do believe it refuse to apply it?

The answers are simple: The ideas are contrary to human nature. The investors bought the stock because they believed it would go up. They are reluctant to admit a mistake. They act on hopes, not facts.

In my experience, those who refuse to believe that the small loss will ultimately be beneficial are just plain stubborn. They ignore the truth and live in a dream world of hopes.

Those who know this principle to be sound but refuse to accept it make up the majority of losers on Wall Street. They are rigid people who consider

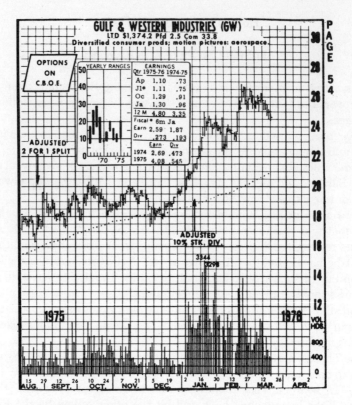

every loss a personal failure. Their ego is more important than their pocket-book. They have a masochistic need to "ride it out," "hang tough" with a stock while it plummets. They cast aside the basis of Blackman Strategy: *The only reason to be in the stock market is to make money.*

It hurts to lose but it won't kill you. What will destroy you and your capital is not facing reality. Taking the loss as I suggest is a healthy financial decision and the sure sign of a winner.

THE MYTH OF A PAPER LOSS

There's no such animal as a paper loss. A dollar bill is paper. A paper loss is a money loss, pure and simple. If you have 300 shares of a stock that drops from 21 to 18, it may not look too bad on paper, but you are $900 poorer.

By not getting out in time, you've destroyed an essential part of successful stock market strategy. You are no longer clearheaded or objective. As you will learn by experience, when you're holding cash, you think more clearly than when you're holding stock.

THE GREEDY INVESTOR

Another reluctant seller is the greedy investor who wants to make "a little more." An illustration is this example: In mid-1974, we recommended Gulf & Western Industries, Inc. (GW). Within a year, the stock went from 9 to 26, then dropped back to 25. At this point, the chart showed a downbreak. Our advice: SELL. (*Note:* This transaction and chart are before stock splits.)

One particularly competent registered representative, a 20-year veteran, was not convinced. He told me, "Dick, I know that GW had a chart break but what's wrong with the company?"

He felt that he should sell but, from reading the newspapers and company reports, saw that everything looked so good that he couldn't believe there was any deterioration in the company's prospects. It was difficult for him to accept the fact that drawing a line on a piece of paper meant the stock had reversed its profitable trend and was now becoming a down stock. He also knew that some of his clients who had just bought the stock would be upset. Only a few days before, his recommendation had been to buy.

I told him, "Either we believe in technical analysis or we don't. I do believe in it. The chart shows that there is something wrong: maybe the rate of growth will be slowing, since it's a cyclical stock. We won't know the fundamental answer for three to six months. Let's not wait for the next quarterly report to discover their problems."

It was not easy, but we both acted on the chart break and sold. Once

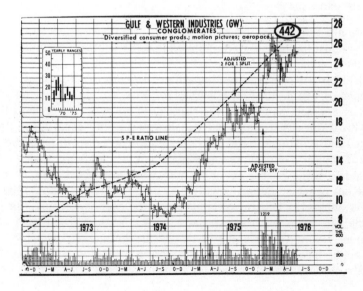

again, the chart was correct. Right after our sales at 25, a large block of stock, 600,000 shares, came across the tape. The next day there was a 200,000-share trade at 24.

At this point the RR began to feel better. He had relearned two essential lessons: (1) The chart does not lie; (2) Sometimes it's necessary to take a loss reluctantly to survive in the stock market.

The clients who bought GW at 9 made substantial profits. Those who came in later, up to 22, made less but did not sustain the losses that they would have had if they held on while the stock dropped, eventually to about 15.

This was a difficult decision for the RR. He did not want to appear to be churning the accounts of the late buyers or to admit that the buy recommendation had been wrong. It was tough to tell a client who had owned the issue for only a few weeks to liquidate. And it bruised his ego. But the results were wise, and in most cases profitable.

TRENDS WITHIN TRENDS

When there's a break in a minor uptrend, the stock will stall temporarily (G&W in January 1976) and may even fall back to the bottom of the up channel (early February). As long as there is no significant breakthrough there will be a recovery and a further drive upward (late February). This may be due to the overall market or to hesitation about the company's future. In both cases, these are trends within a trend. There was, and is, no reason to panic.

There are times when everyone, no matter how experienced or talented, finds it almost impossible to discipline himself to obey this simple rule: *Sell when the uptrend line is broken.*

Such decisions can be upsetting. Often, I *know* that tomorrow the stock will move up again. But I have learned to force discipline on myself, to obey the chart and sell. Sometimes the stock does go back up—perhaps the next day. This is not easy to take, but I realize that to be successful in the stock market I must maintain basic principles and take the small loss. The preservation of capital is of primary importance.

Once in a while I'll lose out on an unexpected comeback. But I know that, in nine out of ten situations, I will be avoiding a greater loss. At the end of the year, when Uncle Sam wants his taxes, the experienced investor realizes that the big losses are the expensive ones: "Without these two or three whoppers, I would have had a great year in the market." Don't weep over what might have been; cut those big losses by taking small ones fast. In Wall Street it is just as important not to have losses as to make profits.

13.   Myths of Wall Street

Wall Street is famous as the international center of finance and the pulse of American economic life. But it is also a small community that thrives on nonsensical myths and rumors.

If you can stand back and survey the stock market as a human phenomenon and not a cast-in-concrete institution, you can understand why none of the myths are worth a tinker's damn. Personally, in my 16 years in the brokerage business, I have never made a dime by following these shibboleths. As a profit-seeking investor, you should be aware of these myths, use only what is true and timely, and reject the false, dated and dangerous.

Here are some myths that, if followed, will lead into a sucker's game and assure losses:

MYTH #1: WALL STREET ANALYSTS INTERPRET THE NEWS CORRECTLY FOR THE INVESTOR.

This is the Big Lie. Usually you'll make out better if you do the opposite of what Wall Street—and the media—advise. This is the Theory of Contrary Opinion. It has always worked well for me.

The security analysts, brokers, newspaper columnists, market-letter writers and TV newscasters who interpret financial news are nice folks. They make the mistake of believing too much of the stuff they're telling you. In most cases, their "lies" are unintentional. They do not realize how they are being manipulated by powerful forces. They fail to take into account the sources of frequently false (and usually incomplete) information. And, under the pressure of registered representatives or of deadlines, they interpret news glibly and, too often, incorrectly.

The public, acting on this "superior wisdom," buys or sells a stock. The giants have made their point and profits. It's a filthy game, unethical, immoral and costly to the individual investor. The Big Lie works because, as Barnum said, "There's a sucker born every minute."

Here's one classic example:

Howard Hughes, the fabulous recluse, must have studied P. T. Barnum's biography. He out-manipulated the U.S. government, the Wall Street establishment and, of course, the general public. In the early 1960s, the business world watched Hughes fight to retain control of Trans World Airlines, Inc. (TWA). The press was filled with stories noting that "TWA was his baby . . . he was an aviation founding father . . . was in agony over the threat of losing his beloved company . . ." etc.

While this "losing fight" was taking place, TWA stock rose from about 30 to 85. The day of reckoning for "poor Howard" came in 1966 when the courts turned down his last appeal. He was "forced" to sell all his TWA holdings. The stock was distributed, at a hefty commission, by a superlarge brokerage firm, at approximately $85 per share. "Poor, defeated" Mr. Hughes netted a cool $500 million!

During this period, the charts of TWA were flashing sell signals: the number of stock transactions swelled to 400 percent of normal volume and the stock, at the time of distribution, was at the top of a steep one-year UP channel. Both of these were inviolable sell signals.

And "luckily" for Howard, although 1966 was a poor year in the stock market, he did well. The Dow Average went from 995 to 774, the sharpest dip in a decade. TWA did take a temporary plunge but bounced back almost to its previous peak.

After the sale of the monstrous underwriting, the stock soared to a high of 101 (one last chance for the smart operators to cash in). By fall, TWA had dropped to 55. In 1968, despite the strong bull market, the stock was in the mid-30s, and, in steady 1970, fell to 10.

Howard Hughes was "forced" to sell his stock just below its high, all because of the myth that Wall Street analysts are correct, intelligent and savvy!

Always be wary when a story hits the financial headlines: whether in the business section of *The New York Times*, as a feature in the *Daily News* or as a lead commentary on the 11 P.M. TV news. By this time, the revelation is no longer news. The insiders have acted and the market has discounted its effect. Or it could be that the pros are setting you up for another rip-off.

The way to beat this situation is to play the Devil's advocate: to ask yourself, "What if the opposite is true?"

If what they are telling you is a severe problem and will continue for another 18 months, consider the opposite of what these self-styled experts advise.

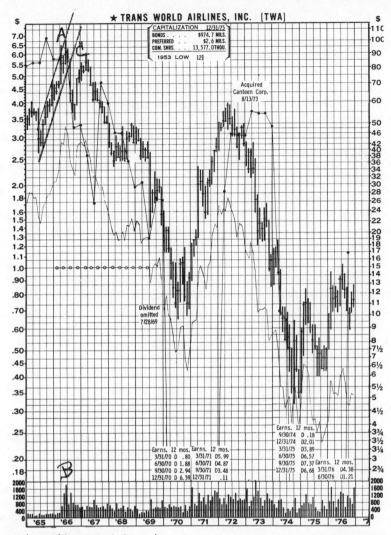

★ TRANS WORLD AIRLINES, INC. (TWA)

CAPITALIZATION 12/31/75
BONDS . . . . $974.7 MILS.
PREFERRED . . $2.6 MILS.
COM. SHRS. . . 13,577.0 THOU.

1953 LOW 12¾

Acquired
Canteen Corp.
8/13/73

Dividend
omitted
7/28/69

Earns. 12 mos.
3/31/70 D .80
6/30/70 D 1.88
9/30/70 D 2.94
12/31/70 D 6.39

Earns. 12 mos.
3/31/71 D5.99
6/30/71 D4.87
9/30/71 D3.48
12/31/71 .11

Earns. 12 mos.
9/30/74 D .18
12/31/74 D2.01
3/31/75 D3.89
6/30/75 D6.57
9/30/75 D7.37
12/31/75 D6.68

Earns. 12 mos.
3/31/76 D4.38
6/30/76 D1.21

A = sold at top of channel

B = heavy volume

C = break in channel

If the opposite of the counsel *is* true, think, "How can I profit?"

You do not have to be a genius to make money on Wall Street if you force yourself to face facts. Keep your eyes open, your ears closed and go against the "accepted" knowledge. Nine out of ten times you will make money.

MORE EXAMPLES OF MISINFORMATION

Here are two more examples of the myth of Believe the Experts: one a domestic news event, the other an international crisis.

Not so long ago, the shrill voices of Wall Street, TV and the press were singing funeral dirges for the U.S. dollar. It was "worthless" and "inflation was running unchecked."

These laments didn't mean a thing. As we now know, the opposite was true. That was the time to hold every dollar and realize that its value was much more than you were led to believe.

Sure, things were tough: between 1970 and 1974, the stock market drop was greater than that of 1929. The value of the average stock fell 70 percent. But that was temporary.

By late 1974, the stock market had bottomed. If you had held your dollars in cash, a minimum of $5,000 invested in bargain stocks would have started you on the road to financial success. You could have acquired stocks on a value basis unseen since 1929 and at prices that probably won't come again for another 30 years. The experts, the institutional money managers and the high rollers didn't panic through this period. They manipulated the bad news to their own interests.

While telling you that your money was worthless, they took their money out of the stock market and put it into fixed-income instruments such as government securities and certificates of deposit. They bought CDs, in minimum units of $100,000, with yields of up to 12 percent.

Meantime, the small investor had to settle for 5 to 6 percent in a savings account or, if he could come up with $10,000, a return of 7.9 percent from Treasury bills.

After the inflation crisis, the law was changed to allow money market funds. These are mutual funds that invest in liquid assets such as government securities, CDs and bankers' acceptances. These new types of investment companies help people with modest capital to take advantage of high interest rates. It was better late than never.

The next time the stock market is getting hit, take your money out and put it into one of these special funds. When the market is going down, money becomes tight and interest rates go up. Copy the pros; sit tight and collect your interest while you wait or go short with all or part of your funds.

CASHING IN ON A CRISIS

The international event that shook the economy and the stock market was the oil crisis. The Dow Average dropped 250 points on news of the embargo; the pundits predicted gas at $1.00 per gallon; Wall Street was sure all hell was going to break loose; and *New York* magazine printed a scenario of American troops "liberating" oil fields in the Middle East.

It may not all have been intentional, but the results were damaging. The small investor was set up like tenpins to accept a big boost in the price of gasoline and sharp curtailment of motoring. The public was told that it would be virtually impossible to take a Sunday ride or even drive a few blocks to get to McDonald's for drive-in food. The motel industry would be a catastrophe, because the traveling sales business was doomed. Etcetera.

With few exceptions, the predictions for stocks were equally dire: industries affected by the oil embargo would be hurt and many companies would be almost driven out of business. It was gloom and doom.

Let's look at what actually happened:

When the oil embargo hit, the Big Lie forced the price of McDonald's stock from the 60s to 21 in six months. Yet, when people realized that they could still drive around, the stock went back to 60—in five months. Today the fast-food chain has not only survived but is raking in record gains.

The traveling salesmen continued to roll. The motel stocks came back. At the outset, they were down 90 percent to 95 percent, more than any other group on the NYSE. This was the time for Contrary Opinion. These shares were the best buys.

That's why I advised my clients to buy Holiday Inn at about 6, down from 55, and Howard Johnson, at 5, down from the low 30s. In both cases corporate profits were off, but percentagewise nowhere near as much as the stocks.

By not accepting a myth of Wall Street and by relying on facts rather than emotion, my clients did well. Earnings of the motel chains snapped back to levels that equaled or exceeded those of 1973. The stocks moved up.

The national picture was just as encouraging. In 1975, the United States reported the largest trade surplus (in excess of $10 billion) of all time.

Moral: Use your common sense. Don't believe the Big Lie.

MYTH #2: YOUR MOTIVE IN THE STOCK MARKET SHOULD BE TO INVEST, NOT TO TRADE.

I say just the opposite: Never invest; only trade.

The objective of investing in the stock market is to make money. If you have lots of money and are young enough, long-term investments can pay off. But if you are like most people, with limited capital and already in your middle years, you should trade for fast, big profits.

One of the standard objections to trading is the tax liability. I never cease to be amazed at the person playing the stock market (and usually, his broker) who insists that his only concern is long-term capital gains because he's afraid of the heavy taxes on short-term profits.

That's foolish and unsupported by facts. A person making $35,000 a year pays federal income taxes at an effective rate of about 20 percent, roughly $7,000 a year. The long-term capital gains tax would be one half of the regular rate, to a maximum, for most people, of 25 percent. Figure out the taxes for yourself.

If you're trading $20,000 and make a profit of $10,000, you would have to come up with $2,000 to $2,500 in taxes. You would still have $7,500 to $8,000 for better living.

Taxes should never be a primary factor in stock investments. Don't be concerned with taxes; *do* be concerned with profits. Make your money and pay your taxes.

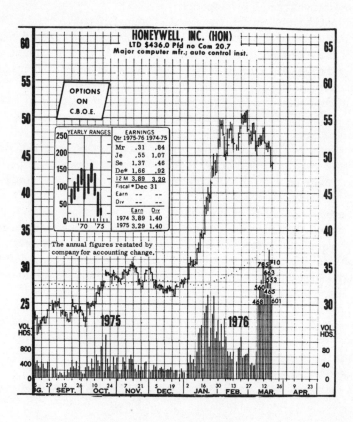

This emphasis on taxes cost two of my largest accounts sizable sums of money. Each was worth in excess of $1 million. Early in 1975, for each account, I bought 1,000 shares of Xerox at 53 and 1,000 shares of Honeywell at 44. Within 60 days, the prices of both issues soared: Xerox to 68 for a profit of $15,000; Honeywell to 57 for a $13,000 gain. (Note how the charts called the shots.)

Both stocks broke the uptrend channel but I did not sell. I was concerned with the tax consequences because both men were in the 70 percent bracket. I wanted to get long-term profits and felt that both stocks would rebound and eventually double in value. I looked for a strong market and did not think either stock would go lower than the price we paid.

But I had become a tax fool. I made the mistake of letting the thought of taxes cancel my ironclad rule of selling when a stock breaks its uptrend channel. When both Xerox and Honeywell went down below their cost prices, one of the clients asked me, "Did it break your rule about channels?"

"Yes, it did," I told him.

"Why didn't we sell? was his next query.

"I thought these stocks were of such good quality and had Big Hit written

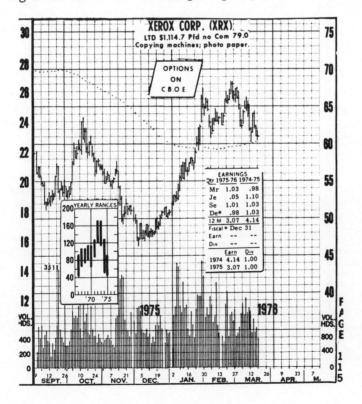

all over them. With long-term gains, the taxes would have been lower," I explained.

"Well," he said emphatically, "what about your principle, 'Take your profits and pay your taxes'?"

I always think of these two clients when I am confronted with tax-related situations. You should, too.

This example illustrates three important points which are stressed throughout this book:
• Always sell when the charts tell you to
• Maintain discipline so you won't be swayed from the chart indication for any reason
• Take your profits when you can and be glad to pay your taxes

BETTER RETURNS WITH TRADING

The best reason to trade rather than to invest is the profit motive: a target of a minimum total return—capital gains and dividends—of 20 percent per deal. This can be achieved sooner (in less than three months) or later (a little over six months). Trading enables you to keep your capital working: to be ever ready for new, profitable opportunities. With investments, you have to hang in there and miss many short-term gains.

Two worthwhile trades a year will bring a 40 percent return. At this rate, you will double your money every 18 months.

(To find out how long it takes to double your money at any fixed rate, apply the rule of 72: Divide the rate of return into 72. At 6 percent, it will take 12 years for one dollar to grow to two dollars.)

If you are wise and lucky, the total returns of long-term stock *investments* will average about 10 percent a year. That means you double your money in a little over seven years: four times as long a period as with *trading*.

If you put your money in a savings bank, at 7 percent interest, the doubling will take a shade over ten years: $72 \div 7 = 10.2$.

If your investments in the stock market cannot achieve returns substantially better than those of a safe savings account, why take the risks?

But if you do want to make money, don't invest—trade.

MYTH #3: STOP ORDERS WORK. ALWAYS USE THEM.

This is not true. *Buy* stop orders work; *sell* stop orders don't.

A stop order is an instruction to your broker to sell at the market price when a specific stock hits a predetermined point.

That is, you buy a stock at 50 and, fearful of a decline, want to cut your losses, so you set a sell stop order at 47½. At this price, the stop order becomes a market order. If your stock declines to, or below, 47½, your position is supposed to be liquidated with the small 2½-point loss.

The trouble is that this stop system seldom works. In a down market, a stock will slide past your price, and since the specialist is obligated to get the best first market price, you may be lucky to end up with 46!

Another problem is that the specialist may violate the regulations of the New York Stock Exchange. He will be fined but you lose money.

In the example above, you have a sell stop order in at 47½. On his book, the specialist has four other such orders: 700 shares at 47; 100 shares at 46½; 100 at 46⅜ and a big one, for 2,400 shares, at 46.

Under NYSE rules, once the stock reaches 47½, the specialist must sell the stock at whatever level the market price happens to be. *Example:* The stock closes at 48⅛. The next day, the first bid is 46. Because the market is weak, the specialist decides that this is the right price to start trading. He fills all of the orders at 46. The stockholders, except for the last one, collect considerably less than they anticipated when they set their sell stop orders.

The specialist might be fined, not for missing the stop orders, but for failing to maintain an orderly market. NYSE officials might rule that the specialist set the opening price too low and that, by buying shares at that price for his own account, he triggered the sell stop orders.

Sell stop orders are never used by professionals, only by gullible amateurs.

Another reason why sell stops don't work is that individual investors have little faith in them. They feel they're cornering themselves into a defeatist attitude and, therefore will continue to lower their pre-set selling points. Here's a real life case history:

A client of mine, who had been an officer of a large drug corporation, made enough money to retire, thanks to an executive stock option program. He started playing the stock market with some $800,000. By the time he came to our firm, in late 1974, his capital had been drilled down to $100,000.

When I explained my theories, he said, "Look, I'm a big boy and don't want this account on a discretionary basis. I will use my own theories. I've got to have the last word."

In January 1975, when the market was hot, we started trading. He made money right away. With a margined $200,000, he concentrated in eight or nine stocks (more than I recommended). Sad to say, this concentration was the only sensible strategy he followed.

Between January and May, we built his equity from $100,000 to $190,000. The rough days came when the market was rocked with broken trendlines. To my mind, he *had* to sell to protect his profits. He had no reason to worry about taxes because he had been taken to the cleaners for over $700,000.

At one of our typically stormy conferences, I warned, "The market is nearing a top. It may have a couple of months to go but it's definitely nearing a peak. While you're sitting on your hands, those strong stocks we've been trading are getting close to a break. I suggest you listen to me and follow a technique that will make you some money. Any time a stock breaks a trendline, it must be sold. Take your profit and keep it."

He replied, "I disagree with that uptrend nonsense completely. I didn't hire you to tell me when to sell stocks. I've got my own techniques."

With great reluctance, I went along and told him, "OK, it's your money and you're the boss."

He countered my suggestion to sell on uptrend signals by setting sell stop orders. When I reported a sell signal on a stock's chart, he would place stop orders about 10 percent below the price at which each stock broke its channel. He was guessing how far the market would drop while continuing to believe that the stock market would be bullish.

Trendlines meant nothing to him. I tried to explain that all chart configurations were tools, not a gypsy's crystal ball. A break in an uptrendline shows that a stock is no longer an UP stock. When this happens, I want to sell out as quickly as I can.

I purchased one stock for him at 57. It went up 15 points. This was an ideal situation to take profits. He refused to sell and entered stop orders. Then he canceled them.

The stock dropped, broke through the channel but we still had a 12-point profit. He wouldn't sell. Eventually when he did give up, he took a two-point loss. His capital was $2,000 less rather than $15,000 more.

On July 15, the market charts showed a general sell signal. I liquidated everything. But my sell-stop-happy client would not let go. By August, he was whipped. The equity in his account was down to $120,000. He had forgotten that the only reason to be in the stock market was to make profits and to keep them. With technical analysis, he had seen the charts break and other general sell signals. But he could not accept these facts. He lost money because he had no strategy, no discipline, and had bought the myth that sell stops work.

Here's another illustration of how sell stops can hurt. In early 1976, Litton Industries stock was very strong. It broke out of a long consolidation area of from about 6½ to 9, crossed 10 with extraordinarily high volume and went, almost nonstop, to 17. Institutions were trading the stock and, as indicated by the 100- and 200-share lots on the tape, the public was buying, too.

Backtracking started in the 16–17 range, and two days later the stock declined. Now, most professionals guessed that there were thousands of stop orders, placed by small investors, to sell at around 14. They knew that whenever there is a large block of stock, the market tends to move toward the block price, whether the trend is up or down. In this case, the large block was the total of the sell stop orders.

Sure enough, Litton traded down to 14¼, then to 14⅛ and, on one sale, to 14. On March 9, at the market's closing bell, came the crusher: 13⅞ on an over-50,000-share block. The sell stops had been wiped out.

The stock should have been sold at 16–17 because of the violation of sell rules. Small investors could have gotten out easily and profitably.

The next morning the stock snapped back to the 15½ level. Obviously the public had been suckered in by the pros. Without a sell stop, at about 14, the shrewd trader could have waited less than 24 hours to boost his income substantially.

Officially it's illegal for the stock specialist to reveal any orders on his book, but somehow this information leaks out, especially to institutional money managers and large individual traders. With such inside assurance, the Big Boys can buy or sell their tens of thousands of shares on scale: in relatively small lots to average in and average out.

Never place sell stop orders that will be put on the specialist's book. Watch the stock action yourself or let your broker do it for you. Such personal surveillance will increase the probability of your being able to sell at higher prices.

Here's what can happen:

Institution X gives an order to its buying broker to purchase at market 10,000 shares of a certain stock which is not held in its portfolios, and to buy on scale down (at ever lower prices). The price of the stock is around 47/48. The broker finds out that there are stop orders set between 45 and 44.

While the stock drifts down, the brokers sit there with a bushel basket. They stay "in the crowd" and buy the stock when it's getting hit and still going down. The drop will start around 48, then accelerate with the stop orders when it gets to 45. Once the institutions have bought their fill at these bargain prices, the stock will bounce back to 48.

The puzzled seller asks his broker, "What happened?"

The answer: "That's the risky thing about stops."

My comment: "A sell stop order is a risk I cannot afford to take."

BUY STOPS ARE OK

Buy stops are usually a good bet. I use them when a stock is near or at a new high: for the year or, better, for all time. Institutions love to buy stocks at new highs. They know that new highs beget new highs—usually.

Sometimes it is possible to trigger the institutions into breaking a stock into a new high by means of a market order or a buy stop. Here's how:

In 1976, I used buy stops with four key stocks: American Telephone, General Motors, IBM and U.S. Steel. All of these touched new highs.

In January, GM moved to an interim high of 60¼. I put a buy stop in at 60¾. This was arbitrary, as it could have been 60⅝ or even 61, if I was optimistic in a strong market.

When the stock went through the new high, the buy stop order became a market order. This is when the institutions came in and powered the stock up so I could sell at a modest, quick profit, at, say, 65. Buy stops put you into a position to catch that line drive. They are also useful to create a good investing frame of mind (which most individuals need more than anything else).

MYTH #4: YOU SHOULD BELIEVE ALL CORPORATE REPORTS ON EARNINGS ESTIMATES FROM BROKERS AND PUBLIC RELATIONS FIRMS.

This is preposterous. It is a subtle form of the Big Lie. The people who issue such news may not even know that the information, in many cases, is erroneous or at best incomplete. Whether they are security analysts or PR agents, they have to rely on statements from corporate officers who, too often, are more interested in boosting the stock than in providing facts.

Estimates of earnings are important to Wall Street. The key element in fundamental research is the rate of growth in corporate profits, especially that which can be expected in the next 12–24 months.

When the analysts projected that per share earnings of Eli Lilly for 1975 would be only a fraction ahead of the $2.59 per share of the year before, the price of the stock plummeted from the 80s to a low of 47.

Conversely, RCA stock bounded up from 19 to close to 30 when estimates indicated that per share profits would rise from $1.63 in 1975 to about $2.25 in 1976.

One of the favorite games of analysts is to guess future profits. That's exciting reading but it is seldom useful by itself. The real value of an earnings projection is as a base for your own judgment. You can do this with quality companies because, broadly speaking, their past records can be projected to future estimates (i.e., if a company has increased its earnings by an average of 10 percent a year for the past decade, it's logical to assume that this pace can be maintained except under abnormal business conditions). Or, better yet, rely on a consensus such as is available in S&P's Earnings Forecast (see Glossary). Use this only as a frame of reference, not as a "guaranteed" projection.

The spread in earnings can make a great difference in the projected price of a stock. The estimates can vary as much as 20 percent: $5.00 vs. $4.00 per share. When a stock is selling at a fairly high price/earnings ratio, say, at 20 times earnings, the hoped-for price could be 100 or 80—a whale of a difference.

IMPORTANCE OF TECHNICAL ANALYSIS

I believe the best way to handle financial information is to listen to technicians, not fundamentalists. This is especially important when there's disagreement on the merits and prospects of a particular company or group.

The fundamentalist always has an excuse. If he's wrong, he'll say, "I'm sorry but my estimates were in error because of blah, blah and blah. Someone else knew more than I did." And he will go on to his next pontification.

Who cares? Whether the reasons were real or specious, it doesn't matter. He was wrong and you lost money.

It's like a lawyer's estimate of a client's situation after the case is lost. The client got stung and all the attorney says is, "What can I say after I say I'm sorry?" The lawyer was paid for performing a task and the client paid the bill.

The real point of these comments is that the analyst, PR man or fundamentalist is not at fault. *The client is wrong for listening.*

If you follow technical analysis, you can count on final, decisive, accurate advice. Charts are impersonal. They reduce the highly variable and dangerous human element. They deal with the most important investment fact: the price of the individual stock at a certain point of time. Such information provides the investor with the opportunity to watch current trends, and project future ones.

MYTH #5: THERE ARE NO GOOD SELLERS ON WALL STREET.

Nonsense. I am a good seller and so are many of my clients. I became a good seller because I kept my losses to a minimum and stretched my profits.

At the end of each year, what counts is not necessarily how much you made in the stock market but what you did not lose. Wise selling is the key to maximum profits and minimum losses. That's why I call this a "selling" book.

To a professional, any profit, large or small, is the name of the game. Whether he trades $10,000 or $500,000, a profit is a profit. He is never afraid to take his gains. And while he pays attention to the chart, he does not neglect any gut feeling that the stock he owns has had it and is not going up. He sells and looks for new opportunities.

I am considered a good seller because I obey my own rules. It is never easy to maintain such discipline, but in selling it is essential. Holding onto a declining stock is like fighting a forest fire in a 30-mile-an-hour wind. The only thing you can do is to get out: as fast as you can.

Without technical analysis, knowing when to sell is difficult. With charts, that selling decision may not always be easy, but it's loud and clear, and 90 percent of the time it is correct.

MYTH #6: QUALITY OF STOCKS IS A SECONDARY CONSIDERATION IN BUYING FOR TRADING.

Stocks are simply vehicles. For the best ride, you can't beat a luxury car. The same philosophy holds for investing: Buy the highest quality stocks you can find.

Three of the most important reasons for purchasing only quality securities are:

1. *Similar costs:* Whether you buy and sell quality or junk stocks, the commissions are the same;

2. *Lower risks:* When you hold stocks of well-managed, financially strong, profitable corporations, you know that you are in good company. Millions of shares are held by institutional investors. This provides liquidity in the market and a continuing check on managerial competence. Corporate executives must produce or be replaced. And, with some exceptions, these companies are so huge and dominant that the chances of unexpected, upsetting events are small.

3. *Concentration:* With quality stocks, you can afford to put all of your money in a few stocks. This concept is basic to Blackman Strategy.

Throughout my brokerage career, I have advised small investors to concentrate their capital in one stock with which they can feel comfortable and sleep soundly. More important, I've found that this principle makes money.

Every businessman will tell you that most of his profits come from a few product lines. The rest of the items, whether it's manufacturing or retailing, carry the overhead, add volume, but do not contribute so substantially to profits.

It's the same with stocks. Your big profits come from one or two Big Hits. If you are skeptical, check your own portfolio for the past few years!

Many times, that one stock I suggested was IBM. If you have $5,000 and IBM is at 200, you can buy 25 shares. If the stock goes to 250 (and that's not an extraordinary swing), you've made 50 points or $1,250 on your $5,000 investment.

You do better if you are margined. At 50 percent, you can buy 50 shares of IBM and get a $2,500 gain: 50 percent on your money. IBM is consistent and acts in harmony with the general stock market. When the overall trend is UP, IBM is usually an UP stock. As long as this move continues, I will urge all accounts to concentrate their capital. To make the Big Hit that will build your capital, pick a quality stock, invest heavily and watch the charts.

MYTH #7: DIVERSIFICATION IS GOOD FOR THE SMALL INVESTOR.

I believe the opposite is true. Not only is such strategy unwise for the small investor but it can wipe him out.

There are two major reasons for this strong contrary opinion: costs and potential profits.

Commissions are expensive. On a $10,000 to $20,000 account, diversification will boost trading costs way above those of concentrated buying: as much as 500 percent more if you buy in odd lots. With out-of-pocket brokerage fees of 8 to 9 percent on both sides of scores of deals, it's difficult to make money and increase your capital. The higher your single investment, the lower your costs. By buying 500 shares of one stock rather than 100 shares of five companies, you can cut your transaction fees by as much as 40 percent.

In fact, I feel so strongly on the folly of diversification that if you have your money spread over more than five holdings, my advice is: *Sell all but one immediately*.

As a rule of thumb, I believe that if you have less than $25,000 to invest, you should own one stock, two at the most; with $50,000, two stocks; with $100,000, no more than four. Diversification lessens your gains. You will do better by concentrating on a few issues that look like potential winners than by trying to spread the risk.

Furthermore, the potential profits will be greater because concentration forces you to buy the best-quality stocks. In an UP market, either all groups will be going up simultaneously or one or two industries will be moving cyclically. This is the time to concentrate where the action is most favorable:

• In the chemical group, one of such stalwarts such as Dow, Du Pont, Monsanto or Union Carbide

• If the computers look good, choose Burroughs, IBM, Sperry Rand or Digital Equipment

• If the automotives are bubbling, make that one purchase Ford, General Motors, or possibly Chrysler

This selection technique is logical. Can you picture the stock market going up without Dow, IBM or GM not participating in the rise?

MYTH #8: DON'T WORRY ABOUT THE DECLINE OF YOUR STOCK IF IT'S GOING DOWN ON LIGHT VOLUME.

This is one of Wall Street's favorite myths. Many professionals really believe it. The facts prove otherwise. In recent years, most declines, major or minor, have been accompanied by light volume. Just look at the charts!

The truth is that, in a declining market, a lower price plus lower volume usually means that lower prices are still to come. It can take institutions as long as two years to liquidate their positions.

Look at Eastern Air Lines. In January 1973 there was a clearcut break on fairly heavy volume. The stock continued to drop with ever lower volume. In 1974 and 1975, when it kept falling and bottomed out at just over 3, the trading was comparatively miniscule. Anyone who placed his hopes on the myth of light volume would have been almost wiped out.

Sure, there are fewer sellers when the price drops, but there are also fewer buyers. The primary factor is not volume but—always—price.

What's the difference if your stocks go down on light or heavy trading? You're losing money. Pay no heed to the RR who tells you that on light volume declines are temporary. Next time he suggests this, ask him to give you examples. I'll lay three-to-one odds that he cannot come up with more than a few isolated cases.

When the chart shows a break down through the uptrend line (or any other established formation), forget about volume. Sell. There's little chance of an upmove regardless of activity. The major investors have lost confidence so who's to do the buying to force that fast recovery?

All brokers and investment advisers tell you to be skeptical of tips, inside information and unverified projections. To this good advice, let me add: *Be skeptical of all myths and rely on fundamental and technical analysis* if you want to make money in the stock market. That's the solid basis for making money and finding the Big Hit!

14.   The Big Hit or the Hot Button

Amateur investors, and many so-called professionals, make two costly mistakes: (1) They expect to make money too easily; (2) They listen to hot tips and gossip.

With encouragement from unscrupulous brokers and investment advisers, too many people look for a stock or an option that will double or triple in value in a short time. They dream of repeating the success of buying Polaroid, Xerox or IBM at $2 per share.

Investments do not work out that way. Very, very few people ever scored such profits with these or any other stocks, and if they did, worthwhile gains took years to develop.

• Polaroid was formed in 1937 but its stock, adjusted for splits, did not move above 25 until 1964. Then, within three years, it was up to over 100

• Xerox, which scored a 1972 high of 171, was trading below 30 as late as 1963

• IBM was selling under 100, on an adjusted basis, until 1962 and did not start its meteoric rise until four years later

Success in the stock market takes time: years with long-term holdings; months with shrewd trading under Blackman Strategy.

As for tips, I never cease to be amazed at how gullible normally intelligent people can be when it comes to gambling their savings on an intriguing concept that will "revolutionize" an industry. The most recent example was the West Coast firm that claimed to have a converter that would separate hydrogen gas from plain tap water. Before the SEC halted trading, this stock, listed on the AMEX, went from 2 to 20! Some lucky speculators (and many promoters) did make money but many more people took a beating. In Wall Street, you don't have to go to Aqueduct to find Longshot Larry's touting miracles.

Sure, there will be new Polaroids in the future, and a rare handful of .

145

shrewd, patient investors will make a lot of money. But the odds of sudden success in the stock market are about the same as the odds that you can locate a screen door in a submarine.

Put away your tout sheet, turn out the light on your crystal ball and learn about something to go to the bank with: *the line-drive stock.* It's real, 100 percent legitimate and almost always profitable.

With Blackman Strategy, every review, every study, every decision and every technique is directed toward one goal: FINDING THAT LINE-DRIVE STOCK. This is my hot button: a stock with which I can make a really Big Hit.

By my definition, a line-drive stock is one that goes up at least 20 percent without a significant correction. With your investment margined at 50 percent, you can make 40 percent on your capital. Hopefully, you can score in a relatively short time, no more than three months.

These line-drive stocks are not as difficult to find as the proverbial needle in a haystack or even another stock like Polaroid. You can discover them in every bull market and, with extra research, in many indecisive periods. These potentially Big Hits are the core of almost every UP market. At times, it seems that if they had teeth they would bite you.

There's no secret formula. First, you use technical and fundamental analysis to pick the stocks and then rely on technical analysis to spot your timing. Anyone can find a line-drive stock when he/she has a good understanding of what the institutions are doing or are likely to do. The big investors create these winners. When they make up their minds to buy, their huge resources drive up the price with ever higher volume. The greater their interest, the faster and higher the price movement. These professionals want to make 25 percent to 50 percent, and they can afford to wait a year or two to do so.

The individual investor should make his money in the early stages of this buying boom. You can do this because most of the time the Big Boys are the sole force. With their herd instinct and buying power, they stampede into the stock and drive it almost straight up. Usually the corrections will be minor and temporary.

The key to the Big Hit is to know what the institutions are thinking and quickly to follow what they are doing. When the time is right, as shown by technical analysis of charts, volume, averages, etc., move in with the professionals, or better, start buying early and let them do the powering up for you.

Such playing-the-market strategy does involve some risks. You may be wrong: conditions may change in the market, the industry, the company or the economy. But you still can count on an excellent fallback protection that is not available to the large investors—you have liquidity. If you made a mistake, you can move out quickly with a small, fast loss.

HOW TO FIND LINE-DRIVE STOCKS

The place to start your search for the Big Hit is in the financial pages. Then move to your chart books: first, those of the overall market; then, those of industry groups; finally, to those of specific stocks that are in the news. That's what I do every weekend, as detailed earlier. With a little experience you'll be able to spot potential winners before your broker does.

Throughout this book are charts showing what a line-drive looks like, how it begins, how it behaves and how you can profit. Every chart is worth close study, not only to reveal the history of each stock but also to point up the cyclical nature of the economy and industry groups. Very few stocks move differently from those of their competitors.

Remember: the stock market always runs in cycles. If you are patient and alert, you'll get a chance to ride the wheel up and not be ground under by it. That's one of the most important concepts of Blackman Strategy and one of the surest and most effective ways to make money by trading.

The stocks that attract institutions for that stampede in—and that equally turbulent desertion—are those of the major corporations that meet standards of quality, financial strength, profitability, broad ownership and technical action. These are the holdings the Big Boys want. They know that when they put their weight into such stocks, their compatriots will see the same values and chart signals and will knock down the corral to acquire them. The professional money manager never wants to be caught too far behind by buying or selling too late.

For your own trading profits, you should already be there, or close behind. Whether you are an aggressive or a conservative investor, I believe it's essential that you get your piece of the action resulting from a rising trend in the market generally and the selected stock specifically. A line-drive stock is always an UP stock in an UP group in an UP market.

Be cautious, especially when you have achieved substantial gains. A line drive cannot go on forever. Every stock will have a correction, usually comparatively small. For traders this provides extra opportunities for profits.

A typical example is Litton Industries. The investor who put sell stops in at 14 was stopped out at 13⅞, but the stock rebounded to 16. Those who did not get out in the 16–17 range had to decide whether Litton was still an UP stock that would experience a normal correction or whether it was finished. Such decisions are never easy. This type of know-how improves with experience.

Warning: Don't react too quickly when your line-drive stock price falls slightly below the uptrend channel line. A small decline is OK—but when the drop is 3 percent below the signal point, do *not* buy. Three percent is a large enough downside breakthrough to indicate that there's probably trouble ahead.

Furthermore, a slight drop may be a come-on set up by a major institution that wants to buy the stock and sees a chance to get in at bargain prices. Such a setup can be made by a latecomer. Remember: All institutions use charts.

This is what can happen: The professional money manager is convinced that PDQ is a line-drive stock and can go to 40 from its present price of 33, which, in turn, is up from 30. The stock has been traded heavily and the fund manager has just gotten around to recognizing the potential.

From the tape, he sees a temporary dip to 32¾ and then to 32½. He decides to set his trap. Near closing time, he orders one broker to sell 500 shares at market, and, a few minutes later, he places another order, with another broker, to sell 300 shares at 32.

The first order is executed at 32¼ and the second on target. Now the stock shows a loss for the day. This worries some nervous traders, who make up their minds to sell at the opening. Sure enough, the first sale is at 32 and probably is followed by an even lower price. At this point the professional starts to move in and, by day's end, has accumulated quite a block at a savings of as much as a point a share. That's a lot of money when thousands of shares are involved.

In the same way, the professionals will try to break an uptrend. The Go-Get-'Em Fund decides to buy 100,000 shares of Whistle Stop Instruments, which has moved from 40 to 43 and is now in new, high ground. The fund manager sells 5,000 shares of WSI in 1,000-share lots through several different brokers. By timing these sales, he is able to drop the stock price back to 41⅛.

At this point, Go-Get-'Em starts buying and tells his brokers to get best price "as long as it is not over 42." Such shrewd trading has reduced the fund's acquisition cost.

Added warning: As the trendline becomes a more accepted tool, it's possible that some investors will try to manipulate the data that show up on charts. That's why it's wise to wait for confirmation.

SELL INTO STRENGTH

It is always a good idea to try to sell into strength: i.e., in an UP market with rising volume. This will assure a better price. This means not waiting for a correction and selling too soon. Occasionally, of course, you will miss out on a later rise, but you will avoid agonizing decisions and keep your head clear to determine whether, and when, to buy back the stock in a correction.

With all line-drive stocks, you have two choices:

• To buy for the long-term and hold through temporary fluctuations until you have your 20 percent profit

• To trade to boost your profits: selling at the top of channels and buying at the bottom. Your per transaction profits will be smaller and your commission costs greater than if you had maintained your position. But you will realize extra profits: 10 percent to 20 percent on outright purchases; 20 percent to 40 percent if you are on 50 percent margin

When you trade with a real line-drive stock, you eliminate the crisis decision as whether or not to sell during a decline. You can play the channels and uptrend lines on the charts and continue to make substantial and usually consistent, profits.

To make the Big Hit, wait for an UP market. Then find an UP group and, using your charts, an UP stock.

Don't be afraid to start buying slowly: 100 shares at the start, then 200 or

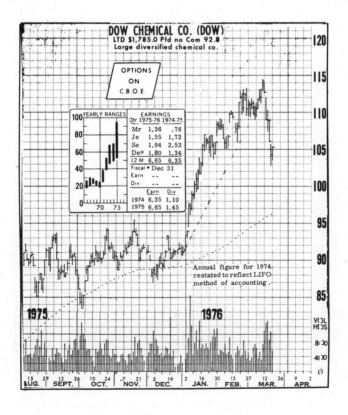

more as the line-drive stock moves up. If you're wrong about the stock or the market, you can get out with a small loss.

But as soon as you feel you're right, move in hard and completely. Concentrate your investment and watch the chart. You are buying high and selling higher.

If you're trading, hold off until there's a temporary dip to the bottom of the channel line. You're after the Big Hit, so press the Hot Button.

ALWAYS PROFITS WITH LINE-DRIVE STOCK

With Blackman Strategy you don't have to catch a line-drive stock early to make money. There can be adequate profits even though the stock has already moved up a long way.

This was the situation with Dow Chemical Co. (DOW) in early 1976. (Note: all prices are before the 2-for-1 split in June 1976.)

The stock had been sensational in recent years: up from an adjusted price

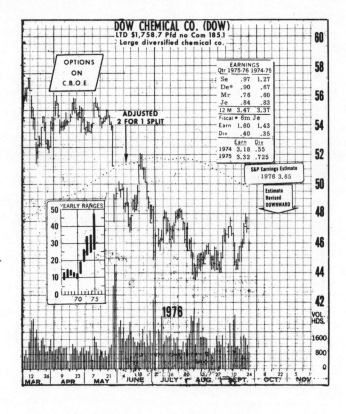

of around 20 in 1970 to the mid-60s in 1974. I traded successfully and, in January 1975, sold into strength when the price was in the mid-80s.

As often happens with winners, I kept watching DOW but did not go back until January 1976. This time the market was strong, and the stock move had been so sharp that it looked like the start of another line drive, possibly to another all-time high.

I was skeptical. The value of this quality issue had quintupled in six years, so could it continue? I decided to follow my own advice.

As I've said before, once you have found an UP stock, check the industry. If the group trend is UP, keep looking; if it's neutral, keep watch; if it's DOWN, forget the stock no matter how alluring.

When the overall outlook is promising, zero in on two or three leading stocks of the industry, not just the one that attracted your attention. Review all of their charts—for 12 years, for recent years and for the past few months.

The chemical industry charts and group action were promising so I looked at American Cyanamid and Du Pont. ACY's movement was OK, but there had been little change over the past year, and while earnings were up, they were not exceptional.

DuPont was acting better but profits had been erratic and generally down. I felt that institutions might not sell but they would not buy heavily either.

DOW looked better all the time. The earnings were impressive: from an adjusted 50 cents a share in 1965 to $2.07 in 1972 to over $6.00 in both 1974 and 1975. Now I had an UP stock in an UP group in an UP market. The potential gain was good, even though more limited than in the past.

I started buying at around 96. The stock continued strong and topped out at 112. This was not quite my targeted 20 percent gain but it came quickly. I did not sell at the peak because I felt there was a chance for a few more points. But when the drive slowed and the uptrend line was clearly broken at 112, I obeyed the chart and sold, in March, at a modest profit.

Over a six-year period, a smart trader would probably have been in and out of DOW four or five times, *always at a profit,* if he paid attention to the charts.

Now let's look at some other theories that have made money for me and my clients.

15. Theories That Work for Me

Throughout my career on Wall Street, I have developed some theories that, when applied in the right situations, make money for me and my clients. Some of these ideas/techniques are known by every professional on Wall Street; others are accepted only by a handful of thoughtful technicians. All of them are tools to make money. They should be used to keep them from rusting.

These theories grew out of actual situations and personal experience. Some came from reading or conversation with market-wise individuals; others were salvaged from losses; but in most cases, these money-making concepts were the result of step-by-step analysis of successful deals.

1. *The best trading stocks are the best investment stocks. The best investment stocks are the best trading stocks.* Too often the small investor tells me that he can't afford to buy high-quality, high-priced stocks such as General Motors, IBM, Merck, Eastman Kodak or Xerox. He says, "I don't have enough money to pay $75, $100 or $250 per share for any stock." Even people who have as much as $50,000 in the market feel this way. This is foolish and eliminates the probability of substantial profits.

I believe that you cannot afford *not* to buy quality securities. These huge corporations have a powerful influence on the American economy. They are the core of most fiduciary investment portfolios. They are the stocks the institutions buy and hold. If you accept my premise of following the leaders, you will always own shares of top-quality companies and, when appropriate, will trade them profitably.

Not so long ago, the former chairman of General Motors made the statement, "What's good for General Motors is good for the country." It seems to me that he would have been closer to the truth if he had said, "What's good for General Motors is good for the American stock market."

I look at GM and Ford stocks daily, and, when there appear to be changing trends, at Chrysler. Many a time their moves will lead the overall market. This is logical. Automobiles are the largest industrial group in the United States. Our entire economy is directly affected by how well or how poorly this industry performs.

GM is the largest nongovernmental enterprise in the world. GM stock has been, and I believe always will be, one of the bellwethers of the stock market. Watch it and you will have a good idea of what's happening on Wall Street. At some time, every investor should own GM common stock. With proper timing you are almost sure of a profit.

Example: In January 1975, the stock market turned bullish. GM stock, down from a 1973 high of 84 and recovering from a December 1974 low of 28⅜, was around 40. By both fundamental and technical analysis, the stock was a leader and in a strong position to move up when the bull market caught fire. GM was an UP stock in an UP market: the oil crisis had abated; the dollar-a-gallon-for-gasoline bugaboo was being ridiculed, and consumer surveys showed that people were getting ready to buy cars again. Most investors, small and large, intuitively knew that GM stock would climb, even if there was some temporary backing and filling.

Unfortunately, too many people with less than $25,000 were not among the buyers. They were wary of quality stocks and still hoping to break even with some of the secondary issues they had accumulated. They would not listen to reason.

I advised one client with $8,000 to buy 200 shares of GM for cash or 400 shares on margin. He insisted on separating his "good" stocks from his "trading" ones. He did not believe that he could make money trading "good" stocks. He told me that he really wanted to buy GM, but for some reason could not bring himself to get out of junk into quality.

As a result he kept trading throughout the year. Despite the fact that 1975 was one of the best years the stock market ever had, his net profit, after paying out $2,500 in commissions, was a grand total of $64!

This was the same period during which GM hit a new, current high of 59. If he had accepted my theory that investment stocks are the best trading stocks and had bought GM at 40, he would have had a gross profit of $7,600—more than 100 times what he actually made. My firm would have received fewer commissions, but we would have had a happy client.

This small investor learned the hard way that one of the most useful investment techniques is to concentrate capital and never diversify with low-quality issues. For the best profits, in all types of markets, trade only with the best investment stocks.

2. *Trade off a position.* This is a compromise technique that enables you to hold in part of your investment in a stock that looks like a big winner. It's

a way of hedging. You sell off some stock for short-term gains and keep the balance for long-term profits, but not necessarily for tax reasons. Trading off requires an UP stock in an UP market, relies heavily on technical signals, and avoids the tough decision of when to sell out.

This concept evolved from my experience with Beckman Instruments in the mid-1960s. I was striving to find a way that my clients could benefit from the tremendous moves which I thought this quality stock could have. Later I used it successfully with major positions in GM, MCA and Gulf & Western.

These were all situations where proverbial Wall Street wisdom says, "Hold and pray. The stock has a good chance to really go. Don't fool with it." That's often good advice, but success may take a long, long time. It would be more rewarding to trade on the basis of the action shown on charts.

Here's how this technique works: I find a stock that is selling at 40. Analysis shows there's a good chance that it will move up to 50 or 60, with the possibility that it might double to 80. I tell my clients, "Look, this stock could become a Big Hit. I know you are worried about when to sell, so let's buy 400 shares. Keep 200 for the long-term. As long as the stock doesn't violate any uptrend line, keep these shares and hope they will skyrocket.

"But to take advantage of temporary dips, trade the other 200 shares. Since the stock is in an UP channel, we will sell those shares when the stock hits the top of its channel. Then, when it drops back to the bottom of the channel, we'll buy back these same shares and repeat the process. This way we'll be taking profits out of the stock while maintaining our long-term position. You don't have to worry about deciding when to sell out your entire holdings."

We buy at 40 and sell 200 shares when the price reaches 48. With normal fluctuations, the bottom of the channel will be about 44, so we buy back at that price, sell again at 48, or perhaps, at 50. Then we wait for the temporary dip and buy back again at, say, 46. As long as you think a Big Hit is possible, it's psychologically easier to hold 200 rather than 400 shares at 48 when the stock drops to 44. It's tough not to sell at the top of the channel. Trading off eases tension and can provide extra gains.

Your profits will, of course, be cut by the commissions for selling and buying, but even with these costs you should still do well!

Variation of this theory: Another version of this trading-off technique is to take your cost out: i.e., when the price of your stock has doubled, sell half of the shares to get back your original investment and ride your profits on the balance.

3. *Sell on bad news or even the smell of bad news on an individual stock.* This is quite a different approach than the one used in deciding whether to

sell when there is unfavorable general or industry news. In the latter case, it may be wise to follow the traditional advice to be cool, calm and analytical.

With individual stocks, this is not a wise or profitable decision. When there is bad news, or even the smell of bad news, don't argue. *Panic and sell at the market.* Let someone else fight the news and the tape.

In my experience, such prompt action will save you a lot of money. It all gets back to the importance of following the leaders: the big investors. Institutions do not like bad news. They prefer "clean" stocks. They steer clear of "tainted" ones. When they are unsure or unhappy, they get out, regardless of the price. Professional money managers do not want to be caught with any holdings that might be subject to criticism by directors, investors or the press.

By prompt selling on bad news, you will be right most of the time. And you will be saving money because you will be getting out before there's a significant decline in the price of the stock. This is another theory that relies on the basic principle of technical analysis: *Act on what the market does, not on what it should do.*

Here's an example of how and why this theory works:

In June 1975, I took a position in Castle & Cook stock at approximately 16. In the middle of July, the ticker carried news of a bribe scandal and a possible takeover of Central American properties owned by United Brands and Castle & Cook.

I immediately called the home offices of C&C in Honolulu and San Francisco. The president was unavailable, and when I finally got through to

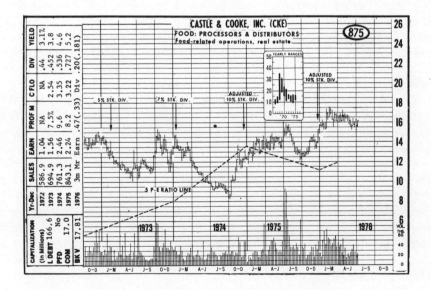

a vice-president to ask for comments on the news, he refused to give a firm denial. He hedged by saying, "We're really not sure. We don't think it's that bad. Within an hour or two, the company will issue a formal statement which will be carried on the wire services."

It seemed obvious to me that the company needed more time to gather people for a meeting to make a decision. I'd smelled smoke and was not about to wait for the fire. I sold out the entire position—my own and my clients'—at about 16½ for a small, fast loss—after costs of commissions.

When the company's statement did hit the wires, it was not a firm denial. Then came a period of indecision in the market, but within the next few months, CKE stock dropped by 25 percent.

By panicking, I was able to get out before the big holders had a chance to drive down the stock price. In Wall Street, when bad news hits a particular company, institutions that hold large blocks of stock almost always hold a group meeting before taking major action. This can take up to two days, but 90 percent of the time the decision will be to sell. Take advantage of this situation and beat them before they start unloading.

BEWARE OF BARGAINS

A corollary of this theory is never to buy a stock when there's been bad news, regardless of how much a bargain it may appear to be.

This is contrary to what most people believe. They assume that the price of a stock declines because of anticipation of bad news, and once the news is out in the open, the downward trend will reverse. This is not true. As short sellers know, and use to profitable advantage in a declining stock, today's low will be tomorrow's high. Remember: a trend in motion continues until it runs out of steam or there is a strong force to change direction.

Take the case of Consolidated Edison. On April 23, 1974, just before the company announced the omission of the dividend, the New York Stock Exchange suspended trading when the stock was selling around 20. A few hours later it reopened at $12.50 per share.

As always happens, the low price attracted bargain hunters. These are the hardy, unsophisticated, unthinking souls who buy on bad news. They kept the stock at the 12–13 level and allowed the institutions to dump their stock (and several portfolio managers to hold their jobs). The clincher came in a few weeks: Con Ed stock dropped to 6! If they held on, they did make money because the stock moved up in the next six months. By heeding the chart, the wise investor would have sold at 12 and bought back in at about 7 when the upmove was confirmed.

4. *Buy the "no news" rally.* The best type of rally is the one that happens without any specific good news. This upmovement is generated by the internal forces of the marketplace itself. This is the time when I buy heaviest.

One of the few times to pay attention to what the analysts, columnists, commentators and your own broker are saying is when the market rallies with heavy volume with no clear reason. Jump in with both feet, because usually these are the strongest and longest-lasting rallies.

The way I see it, you can compare a rally of this sort with a raging river. It is going to go where it wants, and nothing can stop it. The stock market will always fluctuate and move in its own way regardless of news. The most that any news can do is to delay its movement for a few days or weeks. Rely on technical analysis!

5. *Be aware of the 30-point week.* This refers to the movement, up or down, of the Dow Averages in five trading days, Monday through Friday. Usually, this is the maximum number of points a market will move in one week. When this swing comes, it can be an important event that can be used to advantage in timing both buying and selling.

Even in the sharp break caused by the oil crisis, the drop was less than 30 points. But in the big rise in the last week of January 1976, the market zoomed up over 50 points. When something so unusual happens, check the past performance of the market or stock for similar situations. Then assume that history will repeat and take whatever action was successful in the previous periods.

I don't mean that you should pull a general sell when the market goes up 30 points in a week or start buying when the reverse happens. What I am saying is that you should be sensitive to the movement of the Averages in such a short time.

I use the 30-point week as a signpost when I think the market is due for a correction or is at the top of a temporary range. I feel that in an UP market this is the time to take a profit. If I stay longer, I'm liable to get burned. Unless there are strong chart movements to the contrary, I sell.

Conversely, I believe that one of the best times to buy stocks is when the market has dropped more than 30 points within one week. Usually this creates a temporary bottom from which a rally begins. At this point, you can get in at a lower price because most stocks follow the market. But be cautious in a long bear market. That rally may be only a prelude to a further decline. In 95 percent of the situations, this is a signal worth heeding.

6. *Cash in on the 100-point move.* The most rewarding market move is a rise of 100 points. On the first 30 points, the profits are modest, but from then on, it's all money in the bank.

There's no way to know for sure when such a swing will occur, but, with experience, you or your broker can *feel* it coming—with a bit of help from long-term charts. Move in on quality stocks and you'll almost always make a Big Hit.

At the outset, the hardest thing to do is to hang on when you have a substantial profit. As long as the trend is UP, *hold*. The biggest gains will come in the last 50–75 points.

The reverse is true with a 100-point drop. When you rely on charts, you will get out early and fast. Too many people are reluctant to sell, especially when they have accumulated sizable gains. They figure that the market will bounce back. As the charts show, this seldom happens.

This is the time to stress another element of Blackman Strategy: how to keep your money after you make it. Never be afraid to get out and stay out of the market. Or, if the 100-point drop is real, to sell short.

As with the upmove, the first 20-point drop is not usually significant. No one believes the market will plummet. But do not hang in on hope. If the Dow Average or any of my sell rules is violated, sell at the market!

To those who won't believe the charts, the next 20-point dip is scary. Thereafter it's panic, wild selling, and everyone trying to get out as fast as possible. This is the ideal time to sell short.

7. *Watch for round numbers in the Dow Jones Industrial Average.* As the charts show, stock market moves usually begin and end near or right on round numbers: 900, 950, 1,000, etc. Investors, whether small or large, professional or amateur, like to talk about round numbers: "I think the market will move to 950."

Since you and I are, generally speaking, responsible for these round numbers, we should use them. That's easy with technical analysis. It may be psychological, but charts tend to conform to round numbers also. These points provide excellent buy and sell signals. If you like to set targets, choosing round numbers can be useful and profitable.

8. *Three losses and out.* This is such a vital ingredient of my investment philosophy that I do not hesitate to repeat it. If you sustain three losses in a row, whether trading long or short, liquidate your entire account.

These poor results show that you are out of phase with the stock market. It doesn't matter why you are losing. The fact is that you are not meeting your primary objective: TO MAKE MONEY.

Sell out, clear your head and give your broker an opportunity to become objective too. Do *not* listen to anyone (especially your broker) who tells you to keep going. Chances are that your losses will continue. Get totally into cash and stay there for at least a week. This will give you time to establish a new, sound base and to review your failures.

9. *Liquidate your account at least once a year.* This is heresy to most brokers and investment advisers. Yet it is sensible and profitable.

Once a year, get out of the market and watch the parade go by. Wait for strong new buying opportunities. Such drastic action will compel you to use proper techniques in acquiring the best possible stocks.

Unless you are a genius, you won't make money every month, and there are no reliable statistics to prove that some months are better for investing than others.

There's no sure way to know the best time to get out, but I liquidate when I feel that the market and my stocks are at or nearing a top. For some people this will be a gut reaction. Others may prefer to use my sell rules.

Another good time to liquidate is when the market is going sideways. As I've stressed, I believe this really means "down." Wall Street calls this a consolidation period. At any rate, it's a time when there's little likelihood that there will be a worthwhile rise.

Critics of this theory will argue that such liquidation is costly in terms of commissions and taxes. I believe the facts will prove otherwise. In most cases, if you can save just one point on every share of stock, you will be well ahead by liquidating. You will avoid paper losses and you will be in a better position to buy wisely because you can pick the best opportunities in quality stocks that are moving up.

In March–April 1974, the Dow Average gave a clear signal when it broke down below 800. I sold and did not consider starting to reinvest until it went below 600 and moved back through 650. I saved myself and my clients a lot of money and worry. And later we scored impressive gains. Look at those trendlines (page 112).

10. *Concentration*. This is such a vital factor in my stock market strategy that I am repeating this basic premise. By concentration, I mean putting your capital in one or two stocks and avoiding diversification.

The marvelous thing about this concept is that you do not have to worry about which stocks to buy. Concentration forces you toward quality stocks and away from junk. With solid, quality holdings, you are almost sure to pick winners most of the time.

And you can sleep well. The risks of large losses are small and there's a good probability that you will make a high percentage gain on all or part of your capital. If you have money in ABC Widget Company, you will worry. There is no way to predict what will happen with small, unseasoned, erratically profitable companies. They are not of interest to the major investors.

By concentration, you will be buying, and trading, high-quality stocks. You will be investing in the issues that attract the major institutions which dominate the stock market.

This should be a continuing process. When you have a winner, keep buying on the way up: 300 shares at 50, 200 at 51, 500 at 52 . . . just as long as there's a potential gain of at least 20 percent and the charts confirm your choice.

On the average, I follow 40 stocks, of which eight or ten will be owned or on the buying list for myself and/or my clients. I concentrate on no more than five stocks with five more in my Reserve List. And, depending on the market and group action, I buy only one or two at a time: always with that 20 percent-profit goal.

11. *Maintain discipline.* As every successful businessman will tell you, there is nothing more important than sticking to rigid rules. This is never easy. It's harder when those rules are contrary to traditional advice and Wall Street concepts.

The Blackman Strategy is based on discipline—on adherence to theories that are logical, realistic and profitable. Discipline means following uptrend lines exclusively. If you deviate and let human nature and whims come into play, you will lose money. But if you pay attention to my philosophy, if you concentrate your money in quality stocks when they are UP stocks in UP groups in an UP market, and sell when the charts indicate, you will make money—a lot of money.

Part of this discipline means disregard of other chart theories. Few of these programs work more than 50 percent of the time. They tend to disregard the importance of institutional investors and to permit individual interpretations. They do not require discipline.

When properly applied and maintained, my theories will work 80 to 90 percent of the time. This does not mean that you will profit with every investment or trade, but it does mean that you will maximize your profits and minimize your losses. Of course, the chances for human error and unexpected changes always exist.

The key to investment success is DISCIPLINE—DISCIPLINE—DISCIPLINE. Before you commit yourself to my theories, read this book at least twice. Then reread it every six months as you move into active trading.

The Blackman Strategy has worked for me for the past 15 years. I have made money for myself and many clients. But I still review every major principle at least three times every year!

Even though I have memorized the key points, I maintain strict discipline —as a broker and as an investor. Right now I am more than ever convinced of the importance of maintaining discipline with all investments. I *know* that my theories work, because I've never done better in the stock market than while writing this book.

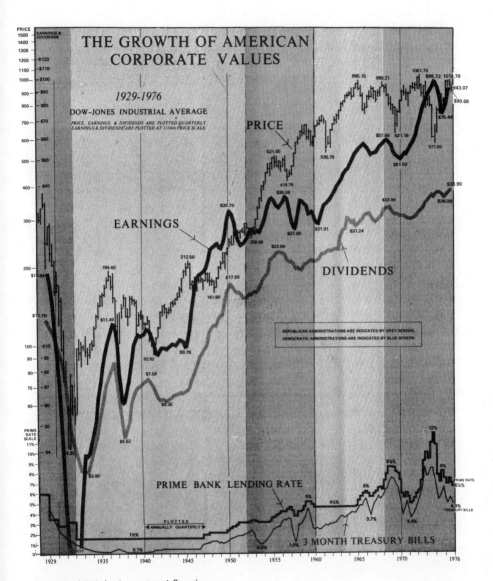

THE GROWTH OF AMERICAN CORPORATE VALUES

1929-1976

DOW-JONES INDUSTRIAL AVERAGE

PRICE, EARNINGS, & DIVIDENDS ARE PLOTTED QUARTERLY.
EARNINGS & DIVIDENDS ARE PLOTTED AT 1/10th PRICE SCALE.

PRICE

EARNINGS

DIVIDENDS

REPUBLICAN ADMINISTRATIONS ARE INDICATED BY GREY SCREEN.
DEMOCRATIC ADMINISTRATIONS ARE INDICATED BY BLUE SCREEN.

PRIME BANK LENDING RATE

3 MONTH TREASURY BILLS

Source: Wright Investors' Service

WHAT IF EVERYONE DOES THIS?

Frequently, after a client has learned to understand (and has profited by) my theories, he will tell me, "Yes, your ideas and practices make all the sense in the world to me. From now on I'm following suit and handling all my investments according to those concepts. I'm tired of losses and happy to be able to chalk up some solid profits for a change."

Later he may ask, "What if everybody follows the charts and the Blackman Strategy?"

My answer: "Don't worry. Change does not happen that fast. Besides, I believe that my theories will work as long as supply and demand are basic factors in the stock market. In a free marketplace, these basic forces will always rule what happens to any product or commodity. You are dealing with quality stocks. You are following the leaders and you are taking advantage of the market as it is, not as it should be. How can you go far wrong by buying an UP stock in an UP group in an UP market?"

Note: As with trading commodities, there are times when special interests will manipulate prices to get just under the uptrend lines to trigger selling. Under such conditions, be flexible and move your buying and selling points out a bit, perhaps as much as 2 percent. My theories are based on supply and demand which cannot be altered. Only the timing of purchases and sales can be manipulated, and then not for long.

16. Worthwhile Investment Maxims

In Wall Street there are a great many maxims. Some of them are false and foolish, but many make sense and are worth following. Here are several adages that will help you to make money in investing:

Don't fight the tape. This is what technical analysis is all about. The new consolidated tape shows the trade-by-trade activity of all NYSE-listed stocks as reported by all major stock exchanges. A good broker will watch the tape carefully to discover what's actually happening in the stock market.

Periodically this information is translated into charts. As a picture of a particular market, the chart tells the truth of what took place in the past. Most of the time the chart can be used to predict the future because markets tend to repeat themselves.

The tape shows what is happening *now*. The NYSE tape runs from 10 A.M. to 4 P.M. and reports prices and volume from moment to moment. Wall Street's "inside information" is as stable as quicksilver. The tape is granite. It shows facts. Trust it. Use it along with charts. Both tell the truth.

Let me repeat: *Never fight the tape.* If the ticker shows a downtrend, do not buy. Conversely, if the prices of the stocks in which you are interested and their related groups move up, get ready to buy. In both cases, wait for confirmation and then rely on the tape, even if you do not fully understand or agree with the trend. This applies to individual stocks and the market as a whole.

Don't average down. That is, don't buy more stock as the price drops. It's intriguing to think that you are building an average price that is lower than your original cost. But what you are really doing is accelerating your losses and making it more difficult to achieve profits.

If you buy 100 shares of a stock at 25 and another 100 shares at 15, your average price will be 20. That's a 25 percent decline. To break even, you will have to get a 33% rise: from 15 to 20.

When a stock starts dropping, the trend is against you. Don't try to rationalize your *buy* decision. You were wrong. Take a quick, fast loss and never average down.

Do buy up. When the price of the stock is going up, keep buying. It's nice to own 300 shares of a stock at 20 and have it go to 22 and find yourself in either a buy or sell position. But with the Blackman Strategy, no stock is ever a hold. As far as I am concerned, if it's a hold, it's a *sell.* When the stock moves up and you decide not to sell, use my concentration principle and buy more.

Always be skeptical. Wall Street myths are sold like snake oil at a medicine show. Do not act on dreams or hopes. Look at the facts and especially the charts. Deal with things as they are, not as you would like them to be.

Be objective and be skeptical. Find out exactly who is giving out information and then examine their motives. Are they institutional managers who want to trap you into a false move that will benefit their portfolios? Advisory services that hope to create promotional records? Or brokers who are anxious for commissions?

Be skeptical until there is solid, factual confirmation from reliable sources and, of course, from the action on the daily charts. Practice discipline. Never be swayed by a grifter's sweet talk or an "expert's" long experience. Trust the charts. They do not care who benefits.

In bear markets, money returns to its rightful owners. What this means is that when the market continues to decline, most people will hang on until the bitter end. When, in desperation, they do sell, the buyers will be shrewd, experienced investors who have access to all the facts. They are the "rightful owners" because they buy on value, not on hope.

It's always up to you to keep your own money. Once that brutish old bear begins to stir in the market, keep your profits by selling promptly. If you're not wily enough to take out the money you've made and run with it, the bear will be more than happy to make lunch out of your losses. When there's a down market, don't try to make money by going long—by holding or buying stocks. Get out, hold cash or its equivalent, or sell short.

Don't try to forecast earnings. In recent years the annual dividends of General Motors have ranged from $3.40 to $5.25 to $2.40 per share. The higher payouts have included year-end extras resulting from improved profits.

If GM cannot predict its financial figures, how can you hope to guess the earnings of a smaller, less stable, less dominant corporation?

Earnings predictions are useful fundamental information. It's best to rely on a consensus such as is available in Standard & Poor's Earnings Forecast (see Glossary).

This monthly booklet lists estimated annual earnings of major corporations as projected by leading organizations. The predictions vary widely: with Diamond Shamrock, for instance, from $6.75 to $8.25 per share. Use a consensus, but rely on the charts for action. These show what the estimators are doing in the market.

Also be skeptical of quarterly earnings reports. They are only estimates. The audit does not usually take place until year end, and, as shown by such disasters as Penn Central and W. T. Grant, this can be the time of truth. Don't forecast; use charts.

17. How to Make Money in a Bear Market
by Selling Short

Selling short is an integral part of Blackman Strategy. It is one of the few ways to make money in a bear market.

Normally an investor buys a stock long in hopes of appreciation. Short selling is just the opposite. You sell a stock at its current price, which you think is high, and hope to make your profit by buying a similar quantity of the same stock at a lower price.

In theory, short sales are more risky than long buys: with a long position, your maximum loss is 100 percent—the full value of your holding; with a short position, you do not own the stock, so your loss could be 1,000 percent if your shorted stock went from 10 up to 110.

In practice, of course, there are no great risks if you pay attention to the rules and are willing to take a quick loss when your projections are wrong.

Short sales are made with borrowed stock as arranged by your broker. The transaction can be carried out only in a margin account. There's no interest to pay but, as long as you control the stock, you are responsible for paying the dividends to the real owner. That's why professional short sellers prefer stocks that pay small or no dividends, or, if they are available, warrants, which never pay dividends.

To most brokers, selling short is risky, improper, and somehow un-American. They say, "It indicates a lack of faith in the U.S. Nice people just do not sell short, especially with well-known stocks. Keep the faith and hold on until there's a recovery."

That's a crock of baloney. My guess is that two thirds of all RRs have never sold short themselves, and half of them have never had a customer who had the intelligence to go with the market and make profits by selling high and buying low.

166

Selling short is a logical, sensible technique. It provides flexibility to any money-making investment program. If you feel, and technical analysis confirms, that there is a downtrend in the market or in a stock, why not take advantage of this probability by selling short? The dollars you make on the downturn will buy just as much as those earned on the upmove.

In January 1973, there were breaks in the uptrend lines of the major averages, so I felt that the stock market was heading lower. I also saw, by the charts, that a number of famous-name, glamour stocks were overpriced

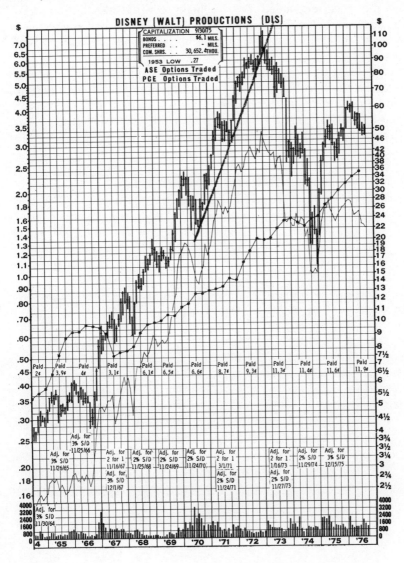

and ready for a sharp downswing. Confirmation came from the drop in the London Index. It was time to start selling short.

A good example of money-making was a short sale of Walt Disney. After a sharp run down from over 120 to 105, the stock climbed back close to its previous high, in anticipation of a stock split. This did not last long. The long, harsh decline started with heavy volume and continued, with some short upswings, until the stock broke 90.

One of my clients sold Disney (DIS) short at 100 and had to sweat it out while the stock rebounded. But he finally covered his position at 95, sold short again at 102 and took his final profit at 90. He had confidence in the charts and sufficient discipline to hang in there. This was a DOWN stock in a DOWN market.

Charts make it easy to find these short-sale candidates. In 30 minutes you can review the weekly charts for the big losers and check their performance against long-term action. See Disney (below), Eastern Air Lines (page 170), Litton Industries (page 63) and even General Motors (page 61).

There are also more subtle points to check:

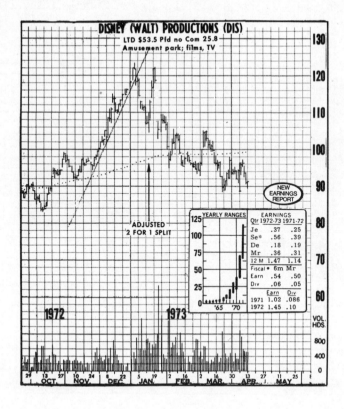

1. *Be as certain as possible that it's a genuine bear market or a major intermediate decline: of at least 75 points on the Dow Jones Industrial Average.*

Use the charts of the major stock markets: the Dow or S&P Industrials for the NYSE and the Financial Times Index for London. Then look for confirmation by a bellwether stock such as General Motors.

Once in a while professional traders will scalp a short trade (take a quick, short profit) when there's a minor correction within a bull market move.

I do not advise this for amateurs. Wait until there's a decisive break down through the uptrend lines of the overall market, then check individual stocks that you feel are most vulnerable. Generally, these will be the downtrending issues which have moved close to, or broken, their trendlines.

2. *Don't try to pick a top*—either for the market or a particular stock. What you want is a sizable, not the maximum, profit. When a stock is making new highs, you don't know whether it will continue to go up. Although it probably will, for a while.

Wait for the formation of a top pattern such as that of Eastern Air Lines in late 1972 (page 170). Or for some other sign of loss of momentum—heavy volume with little price change: Disney in 1972.

Forget fancy patterns. Watch the breaks in the uptrend line. Then wait for a rally and sell short on strength, such as the Eastern bounceback. Very few stocks go straight down at the outset. Most fall, rally and then plummet.

In much the same way, don't worry about timing your purchase at the bottom. If you are still short, watch the chart for a clear reversal: with Eastern this was at about 3½. In most cases you should have taken your profit earlier.

When you are convinced of the downtrend, go short. A trend in motion will continue until there is a strong retardant. And, in most cases, this will not occur until well after the stock has gone below the 20 percent profit mark.

3. *Short stocks that have large institutional ownership and trade in sizable volume.* By this I mean stocks that are likely to be sold in large blocks, 10,000 or more shares. These seldom bounce back very far in technical rallies.

From experience, I can assure you that it's easy to be shaken out of short positions when there are sudden turns against you, even for a brief time. You can get scared and whipsawed with quick fluctuations, especially in lightly traded stocks.

To avoid this possibility, stay away from inactive issues of companies with small capitalization. Let someone else take those risks.

The best stocks to short are quality issues that have become overvalued or whose companies are in trouble. The herd instinct is effective on the downside too. When the institutions stampede, they trigger similar action by their colleagues/competitors. These shifts can be seen on the charts; this, in turn, alerts more of the big investors.

4. *Don't short a stock because you think it's priced too high.* The stock market does not care what you think. There are many things you cannot know about any company. The stock you consider overvalued may be just the one the professionals like because they have inside information.

Example: Eastern Air Lines, in January 1973, made a clean breakout at 22, then dropped almost overnight to 16, its lowest point in six months. It kept falling, went below 11, its lowest value in almost three years, edged up a trifle and, with very small volume, continued down to 3. This weakness was evident in December 1972, months before the decline in the overall market. When a company gets into trouble, price is no object to the Big Boys. They bail out and refuse to consider the stock for years.

5. *Short strong stocks.* This is another example of Contrary Opinion. The prevailing Wall Street "wisdom" is to concentrate short selling in weaker stocks on the theory that they have little support so their prices drop rapidly.

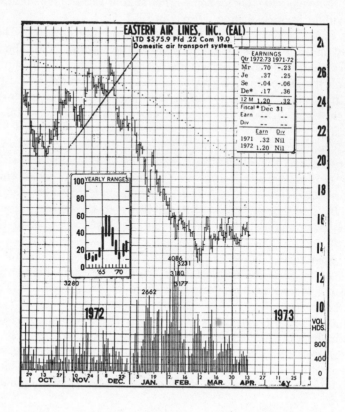

I disagree. I feel that the best stocks to short are those that the institutions don't want: "strong" stocks that are no longer popular. I know that when the pros decide to sell, they are not primarily concerned with price. They want out. As a small investor, you are sure of liquidity and, for some time, can profit from your short position in quality stocks that are being sold out.

Glamour stocks do not break badly until the very end. They resist market declines for a long time. Generally it takes an overall drop of 100 points in the Dow Average to pull down IBM sufficiently to justify a short sale. If you want to sell the big glamours short, wait until the last stages of a bear market when everything is collapsing.

6. *Target your profits*—at about the same 20 percent as used with long positions. At that point you will have a sizable gain and can afford to let the stock keep dropping. If you do buy back and the stock continues down, you can go back and sell short again. You'll feel good, have money in the bank and be ready for more.

7. *Don't let your losses get out of hand.* With long positions, you can let your profits run with an easy mind. You are ahead. Being short involves greater psychological strain, especially when the decline does not come so fast, or so far, as anticipated.

While I do not believe in sell stop orders, I have found that when you are selling short, mental buy stop points can provide welcome protection. If they are violated, close out the trade, take your profit, or loss, and look for other short candidates.

If the stock moves up, not down, I use the same general percentages with short selling as with long buying. A price rise of 4 percent is a signal to get ready to buy back. At an 8 percent upmove, I cover my position. The logic is the same as with UP stocks. I was wrong. I know that it is always better to take a small, fast loss than to hold on in hopes which seldom materialize.

8. *Watch the End of Quarters.* One of the best times to set up short sales is in the last two or three weeks of a calendar quarter: March 31, June 30, September 30 and December 31. This is when the institutions must make their financial reports, which reveal their portfolios.

They do not have to state when they sold a particular stock or at what price. Whether the sale was on March 30 or January 31, the date will not appear in the first-quarter report. The transactions are too mixed for the shareholder to get a clear picture. Someday, perhaps, there will be rules forcing institutional investors to disclose what stocks they own, and when, and at what prices, they were bought and sold.

At the present time, to make a good showing in their portfolios, the institutions start shoveling out weak stocks shortly before the end of a quarter. These are the best stocks to short. The professionals seldom care what prices they get as long as these unpopular holdings are not listed in the public report. This can lead to herd selling: the kind that sent Avon Products from its channel break at 125 down to 18, or Polaroid from around 120 to 14.

This window dressing can work both ways. To improve its performance record, an institution buys heavily in several issues it already owns. This will mean a sudden spurt of two or three points near the end of the reporting quarter.

This gain will usually be temporary, as, a few days later, there will be no more markup buy orders and the stock will drop back to its old level. The institution walks away and the gullible public, attracted by the sharp move, is left holding the bag. The Big Boys can afford to do this, but as an individual you have to enter the next quarter on your own.

This example shows the falsity of that oft-held belief that institutions buy a stock and then support it. Such a situation can occur in a strong bull market but it does not take place in a bear market. Nobody has enough money for this ploy.

Learn all you can about short selling. In bear markets, it is one of the few ways you can be sure of making profits. In volatile markets, it's an important tool for traders seeking quick returns.

18.   The Perils and Profits of Options

Many people have been convinced by commission-seeking brokers and glib financial writers that trading options is a surefire way for the small investor to make a fortune. As with all types of investments, options have perils as well as profits. You can make small, sure gains by writing options on stocks you own. Occasionally you can make solid gains by timing the buying of options correctly. But you can also get badly burned by trading options on stocks you do not own. I am not against options but I do have reservations about their value and use.

First, let's define options. An option is the right to buy or sell a unit of a specified stock (usually 100 shares) at a specified price (the striking price) before a specified date (the expiration date). Options are bought and sold for a premium which varies with the volatility of the stock, the corporate prospects, the size of the dividend, the general activity of the stock market and the price and expiration date of the option. As a general rule, premiums run from about 5 percent for a short-term option on a stable stock to 15 percent for a long-term option on a fast-moving issue.

The most widely traded option is a call: the right to *buy* the underlying stock. A put is the opposite: the right to *sell* the stock. At this time, calls on over 100 listed stocks are traded on the Chicago Board of Options Exchange, the American Stock Exchange, the Pacific Exchange and the Philadelphia Exchange. Trading on a small number of puts has just started.

The two basic types of options trading are selling (writing) and buying. There are variations involving hedging and combinations of calls and/or puts. Generally speaking, writing calls is a sound, conservative way to boost income on stocks you already own. Since you continue to receive the dividends as long as you control the stock, it is possible to obtain returns of 12 percent to 15 percent in a little more than six months on quality stocks: about 10 percent from the premium, the balance from the dividends. By

173

writing calls, you accept a certain, modest return rather than potentially greater appreciation.

I do not write calls because I believe in shooting for maximum gains in minimum time. If I cannot anticipate profits of at least 20 percent in a few months, I keep my savings in the bank. Writing options seldom obtains such total returns in less than one year.

BEWARE OF THE PROMOTERS

What bothers me about trading options are the misconceptions and in- stant-success formulas that con men (and women) have injected into this growing field.

Options are the new game in town, and Americans are always intrigued by something novel. Add the highly promoted "million dollar idea" and you have a magical prescription that many Americans will use, even if they go broke.

As investors, we may think of ourselves as sophisticated, but actually most people can be incredibly naïve. When it comes to the stock market, too many men and women accept premises which have no validity and provide no basis for "How to Make a Million Dollars" or "Guarantee of 40 Percent a Year Profits."

Such misconceptions and instant-success formulas indicate to me that if you're trading options, you should look for professional help from a RR and a firm that has experience, integrity and up-to-the-minute information. Talk to your broker and read the explanatory literature published by the options exchanges.

There is no always-right system for trading options. It's an intricate and ever changing market. If you are not careful, you will lose a good chunk of your capital and may even be wiped out.

Options are just one more investment tool. They are not genies in bottles that will grant you a million-dollar wish. Options should be used carefully, judiciously and properly.

95 PERCENT OF OPTIONS ARE NEVER EXERCISED

Before discussing when to trade options, let's look at some facts. Statistics from the Chicago Board of Options Exchange show that, in 1975, 95 percent of call options were not exercised. Repeat: 95 percent of calls were not picked up because the price of the underlying stock did not score an ade- quate gain.

In April that year, after one of the biggest market rallies in history, only 8.9 percent of all calls were exercised. Obviously, buying calls is not always a successful technique.

This raises the question whether the magic formula for making that fortune may be to short options. Not so. Just talk to the bloodied short sellers after an unexpected rally. Options are as tricky and as unpredictable as the stock market—only more so because their value decreases with time as the expiration date nears.

When you buy options under normal conditions, you are betting that the sellers are wrong and that the price of the stock will rise sharply. Once in a while this happens. But not often, as that 95 percent figure indicates.

What I am trying to say is that, whether it's stocks or options, there is no substitute for hard work, solid fundamental and technical analysis, and discipline, if you want to make money in the stock market. Despite what the books and advisory services claim, there is no easy way to make profits with options all the time.

I get so angry at the hoodwinking of small investors that I want to add another illustration of foolish advice:

One Sunday, in March 1976, I read a research report that stated: "The main reason we have placed emphasis on options during the recent weeks is that we believe that options are the ideal way to invest or hedge during periods of uncertainty, particularly when the intermediate trend is down during an ongoing bull market."

This was, and is, nonsense. It's also highly dangerous. No intelligent investor should buy anything outright when the stock market is going down. I don't care if it's an intermediate trend in a bull market or a full bear market. Logic alone tells you not to buy stocks, but to keep cash.

A corollary of this poor counsel is the investment philosophy widely promoted by banks, brokerage houses and advisory services: "You should always own some securities." Wall Street never wants you to keep your money in the bank.

Let me repeat: The only way you can make money in a down market is to sell short. Buy stocks—and options—only when the market is going UP—UP. If you can't make a profit, stay out of the market—with stocks and options both.

FOOLISH BUYING

With options, it is essential to keep your capital intact. Yet the number of options accounts that have been destroyed or almost wiped out is scandalous. The odds of failure are even higher than they were with the gunslingers of the 1960s. In that hot market, these swingers made a quick profit in one stock but reduced their capital by losses in four other positions. They were wiped out by the eventual bear market.

The new breed of gunslingers are the uninformed and naïve options players of the 1970s. They buy ten options at 3, with $3,000 cash, and expect to make $5,000 to $15,000 within a few months. They must dream of Christmas coming every day . . . or week. This type of naked option buying is outright gambling: unsupported, unrealistic and almost always unprofitable. The commissions will dent you; the losses will kill you.

Here's a case history of such folly:

On March 25, 1976, a client of our firm insisted on buying Merck July 80s. (Each unit is a call on 100 shares of Merck stock at the price of 80 before the end of July.) He paid 3⅜ ($337.50) each when the stock was around $74 a share.

He said that he had "inside information" that Merck would manufacture and distribute the new swine flu vaccine. (Big deal. How could the government not include such a major drug company? And how could anyone expect Merck to make whopping profits from a government-controlled public-service project?)

On June 8, Merck stock was down $67 and the option was trading at $\frac{1}{16}$: 6 cents per call. What he really needed were some profits against which to apply the losses, for tax benefits.

Another trick of options promoters is to urge you to diversify when things begin to look bad. "Spread your options money. Spread your risks," they say.

This is ridiculous. It didn't work for the gunslingers in the new stocks of the 1960s. It won't work for options today.

SPREADING

Keeping in mind that tradable options are a tool to use to make money, you may want to try options spreading. This is really arbitraging. It can be profitable only if you deal in a substantial number of options. Otherwise the commissions can cut deep in the profits.

A spread is a hedge: buying one option and selling another, both of the same stock, at different striking prices or expiration dates. Your goal: to capture at least the difference in premiums and, hopefully, to make a substantial profit if one side moves up or down several points.

Spreads are relatively inexpensive because, under present margin rules, your long (buy) option is adequate to cover the short (sold) option. With a ½-point spread, your total investment is only $50 per spread.

There are two types of spreads: calendar and price. With the former, you trade in options with the same striking price but different expiration dates: i.e., you sell a July 50 call at 3½ and buy an October 50 at 4.

With a price spread, you buy and sell options with the same exercise date but different striking prices: i.e., sell October 50s and buy October 60s with a spread of, say, three points.

With both hedges, the theory is that what you lose on one position, you will make up as much, and hopefully more, on the other.

For my money, these are exercises in futility. You tie up your money for a long time, seldom make more than a small profit, and temporarily lose control of your holdings.

With larger positions in all types of options trading, the commissions are lower percentagewise. You may make slightly better profits but not that 40 percent promised by the hucksters. As in all forms of arbitrage, timing is important. This requires expertise. At my firm we encourage all clients to allow our options money manager to aid, and often to direct, the account.

PROBLEMS WITH OPTIONS

When you buy options, there are always problems that can reduce or eliminate profits:
- If the premiums are too high, the profits will be small;
- If you buy near the top, it means that other people are selling and will not be buyers again;
- There is always time erosion: the closer to the expiration date, the lower the time premium. This can mean a drop of half a point or more in six weeks;
- Options do not always move with the price of the stock. When Halliburton was moving up from 61, I bought options when the stock was in the 63–64 range. I was right about the stock, which topped at 69, but the value of the option remained unchanged until the stock fell to 68, when I sold. I had thought I was being smart and would use the low cost of the option for a quick profit. If I had had to pay commissions, I would have lost money.
- The prices of options can move too fast, even for an on-the-spot trader like myself. If the price of the underlying stock drops one point, the option may fall half a point. This can happen so quickly that you can't get out and will lose a large percentage of your capital.

Example: I bought ten calls at 2½ at a cost of $2,500. I felt that they would rise to 3½ or 4. I was wrong. At 2, I lost $500, or 20 percent of my capital; at 1½, I was out $1,000—40 percent of my investment. If I could lose so much so quickly, think how much more a nonprofessional will suffer!

DOS AND DON'TS IN BUYING OPTIONS

DO *consider buying options only when the market is getting ready for a 75-100 point* UP *move.* This may happen two or three times a year. Even then, the maximum period to hold options is short, usually two to five weeks.

Because of their low prices, options provide greater leverage than do stocks. You get more bang for the buck. But watch the charts carefully. If the UP move doesn't develop quickly, those options can become almost worthless, especially with the loss of the time premium. With all options trading, take your profits fast, pay your taxes and wait for another opportunity.

DO *seek expert assistance.* When I decide that the stock market is ready for a major move, I have a conference with our options manager. I discuss those stocks which, on a fundamental and technical basis, I believe will be the strongest. Then the options manager projects which calls will provide the maximum potential.

If you do buy options, have your RR keep close contact with his firm's specialist. It's a tough field and one that requires more information than is readily available to most investors.

I am never adverse to asking a pro to help me with any investment strategy. I do the technical studies; he does the options projections.

DON'T *trade in the expiration week.* These are the days when both the underlying stocks and the options get clobbered. Trading is especially dangerous when dealing with stocks selling close to their striking prices. There's almost always a battle royal between the options traders in Chicago and the stock traders in New York. The Chicago operators keep selling short in an effort to keep the prices down so that the options will expire worthless. The stock traders buy heavily in an effort to push up the price of the option and make its exercise worthwhile. Stay out of this maelstrom.

SUMMARY

I must admit that, compared to speculating in options, concentrating your capital and waiting for the line-drive stock may seem tame and dull. But the name of the game is profits—not excitement. At year's end, it's not how many times you traded or how much fun you had but HOW MUCH MONEY YOU MADE.

For conservative investors seeking only income, writing options may have merit. But as I see it, the option buyer has as much chance of success as the trifecta bettor. As I understand this horserace deal, you have to pick the winner of the first three races; with options, the trader has to be right on the future of the stock, the time period and the premium.

One final comment: The factors in successful options buying are in direct conflict with Blackman Strategy. When the premiums are small, and thus offer the maximum profit potential, the stock is weak. By the time the chart signals a buy, the premium is usually too high.

19. The Importance of Choosing the Right Broker

The stock market's foundation is not world events, economic philosophy, money or the ticker tape. It is grounded in the everchanging terrain of human personality and psychology. Most successful financiers, and all successful investors, have sensitive antennae for understanding the wants and needs of people.

If you can appreciate the fact that the market is made up of individuals, each with hopes, fears, dreams, knowledge, then you can understand why the client/broker relationship can be one of the most important keys to the door of profits—unless you direct your account and prefer to have your orders executed at the lowest cost.

To be successful with Blackman Strategy, find a broker who believes in technical analysis, keeps charts on his recommended stocks and can call on expert assistance from the firm's research department.

Under all circumstances, remember that the broker is someone you've hired, not vice versa. Listen carefully to what he/she says, but be sure that he/she is listening to you as well. There must be communication based on trust, respect and freedom of expression. If you know and understand this, finding the right broker will not be easy. It will require a thorough, painstaking search and probably some changes. But it will be worthwhile. You will make more money. You will sleep more comfortably.

Here are some ideas to take with you in your hunt for the man or woman who can help you to make your capital grow:

Start your search at a small or medium-size brokerage firm. *Do not waste your time with one of the top ten large wire-service brokerage firms.* Only rarely will a small investor find a good broker in one of these financial supermarkets.

The problem is with the firms, not the individual brokers. By definition, large firms must have corporate policies that are in conflict with the interests of individual investors. The emphasis of these big, national organizations is always on what is profitable for the company, not what will make money for the small customer. There are at least five reasons why this is so:

1. *The registered representative (RR) is forced to sell syndications.* These are underwritings that involve the distribution of securities, usually new issues, but also secondary offerings made by large shareholders. The stocks or bonds are sold by syndicates of investment bankers and brokers who are well paid for their efforts.

The profits from these special deals are 50 percent greater than those of commissions on buying and selling shares of listed securities. Because this income is a prime factor in his remuneration, the RR is seldom able to work hard for you. If you lose money with such a broker, blame yourself for not realizing his personal priorities and the firm's financial emphasis.

Some people will tell you that the underwriting game is legalized larceny. Like all generalities, this is not always correct. But, from my years in Wall Street, I can assure you that it is generally true.

At a huge wire firm, with many branch offices, the broker must push the syndicate business. It's a matter of economics. In most cases, these underwritings account for a large percentage of the RR's income, seldom less than 10 percent, and often as much as 75 percent.

A big firm has more than money at stake in the underwriting game. The research department could damage the corporation's position if it came out with a sell recommendation at or near the time the RRs are trying to persuade customers to buy. Every syndicate member wants the public to acquire the shares in order to insure the firm's guarantee of distribution and to retain the issuing company as a client. A sell recommendation would be a stab in the back and a sure way to end a profitable relationship. Too often, too many brokerage firms move stock on the basis of dishonest, or at least unpublicized, research.

The affirmation of this sharp criticism is that 50 percent of all stock underwritings go down in price, frequently soon after the shares have been distributed and the market support has been withdrawn. Fifty percent may be OK in a horseshoe competition, but in the stock market you'll get clobbered with such odds. With a few exceptions, you'll lose your shirt if you let yourself be persuaded to buy such often overvalued issues!

Stay away from shares of new companies with no track records and therefore no charts to check. If you must consider any underwriting, make sure that it is of shares of an established corporation where the past and recent market action can be seen graphically to guide your decisions.

As is repeated throughout this book, the Blackman Strategy is to buy *only* a stock that is already moving UP. Watch the stock action on the chart. If the issue cannot qualify on a technical basis, forget what the broker, or anyone else, tells you. And pay no attention to the fact that underwritings are sold net (without commission). The truth is that there's a hefty sales charge built into the offering price.

In my experience, some of these giant brokerage firms make Simon Legree look like a humanitarian when it comes to the way they lord over their RRs. Take the story that the vice-president of a wire house told me, only half in jest:

"An office manager, working at night with a group of RRs, informed the assembled group, 'Take your shoes off and pile them on my desk. You don't get them back until you've sold five hundred shares of issue X tonight.'"

Apocryphal? Yes. But I would not put it past some firms. I know RRs who have been forced to work nights. In more than one case, they were told that they couldn't leave until they met their quota.

Other firms are more subtle but just as insidious, to my mind. The manager will tell the RR, "Look, you're not under any quota here. Just work two nights a week, and each night, make at least thirty phone calls. Here's the call sheet. Before you go home, give me a list of the numbers you called and the names of the people you talked to. We want to be sure that you have made every effort to sell this syndicated issue."

That last sentence is the kick in the pants for the RR. He knows that he's got to produce to keep his job!

Now let's look at such situations from the customer's (your) angle. When you come into the brokerage office with your money and explain your needs and hopes, what is the RR to do? Devote time to you? Be interested in your small account?

Forget it. With syndicate profits so much greater than those of commissions on listed securities, the big firm has a powerful incentive to hustle those shares, whether or not they are good investments for the customer.

All Wall Street brokers are on commission, not salary. In the larger firms, the RR is paid 20 percent to 30 percent of the commissions he generates: i.e., if he executes 200 shares at 17½, his gross commissions are about $72. At 25 percent, he gets $18.

Commissions on a syndicated stock can go as high as 9 percent of the value of the transaction. Thus, if your RR sells 200 shares of a special offering at 20, with a credit of $100 per round lot, his gross commission is $200. At 30 percent, he makes $60: over three times as much as with a straight stock deal.

In Wall Street there's no free lunch. You never get anything for nothing.

2. *The research of superlarge brokerage firms is almost worthless to the individual small investor.* He does not, and often cannot, get a valid and timely opinion from such giants:

(a) At some firms, the top researchers are also RRs. Somehow the institutions and other larger clients seem to get the idea to buy or sell first, long before the word becomes public knowledge.

(b) The leaks from government are mere trickles compared to the solid stream from Wall Street. If Woodward and Bernstein wanted to write a book on the stock market, they wouldn't have to work hard to get "inside" information. Although the SEC has strict regulations prohibiting trading stock with such an advantage, leaks are commonplace. They are so widespread and so accepted as facts of stock market life that the rules are almost impossible to enforce. Don't take my word for it. Read what *The Wall Street Journal* said on June 2, 1976:

> S.E.C. sleuths say the process of reconstructing stock-trading patterns to establish insider information violations is time-consuming and often fruitless. It's "an interminable task that few of us relish," one staffer says. The easiest violations to spot, of course, are those causing sudden and noticeable movements in the stock of a company just before a public announcement is made affecting that company. But even after an investigator spots a suspicious-looking trend, it is often difficult to nail down proof.

Some professionals are so calloused and cynical that they have built business by illegal tactics involving non-public information. Again let me quote the same article:

> If you have expertise, you can tell us 100 reasons why you bought a stock without telling us the real reason. . . . People will frequently blame [their trading activity] on rumors in general. They know the burden of proof falls on us to show they had access to material inside information. We know [misuse of inside information] goes on many more times than we can prove.

All this means is that the general public, and thus the small investor, gets the news last, just in time to be played for a sucker by the big buyers or sellers.

With large, national brokerage firms, the recommendations may not reach their thousands of customers for a week or even a month after they have been revealed to institutional money managers.

In small firms, where the research analysts keep close contact with the RR, there's at least a chance that most individual investors will get the word promptly.

3. *Research people of major firms may be forbidden to make valid recommendations for a particular stock.*

One excuse is that "The issue is in registration." This statement is interpreted rather loosely, usually according to how and whether silence can benefit the brokerage house.

The SEC does have a rule that if a firm is presently, or soon will be, an underwriter of a particular issue, there can be no comment. I'm sure that the SEC intended this provision to help the small investor. But, in practice, he's the one who is hurt. "No comment" is not my idea of useful advice.

There can also be a lack of information when the stock is out of registration and available for sale to the public. The silence occurs when the brokerage firm has a "special relationship" with the issuing corporation. That means the corporation is either a present or *prospective* underwriting client. The greater the volume of underwriting by the Wall Street firm, the more "special" becomes this relationship—and the less the flow of research data to small customers.

A smaller brokerage house doesn't have the massive capital needed to support underwriting. Their RRs deal with the public. Their research will be limited, but generally will represent the honest opinion of the analysts who must deal directly with the RRs and be available to answer specific questions from customers.

4. *The partners in a large brokerage firm may own stock, directly or indirectly, in various companies whose stocks are recommended.* Obviously these wealthy men want the public and the institutions to buy and push up their prices.

The plot thickens when the senior partners have large blocks of stock they are not able to sell at a profit. Some of them take advantage of their position to try to boost the stock price by favorable research reports.

5. *Large brokerage firms do not hesitate to put out a buy recommendation to drum up business.* They know that an institutional customer has 100,000 shares of XYZ ready for sale. To throw such a block on the market could be disruptive, and probably, would knock the hell out of the stock price.

Clearly, the portfolio manager will welcome support such as a timely buy recommendation. When the public buy orders come in, the institution will sell into the market the favorable report has created. The broker has "earned" a share of this business.

A variation of this controlled research can be illustrated by a story told by the head of research of one of the major Wall Street firms. During a bad period in the stock market, he was ordered not to give any recommendation to sell General Motors because "It's bad for business."

He was also told "Never be bearish and urge a short sale," even though he personally, and other executives, agreed that the market was going down. They wanted their volume to stay up and couldn't care less about clients. Their theory was that small investors will keep trading, and if they lose, *caveat emptor.*

Later, when the market—and GM—were down even more, the research head was warned again, this time, "Never say 'Put your money in the bank and come back when the market is better.'"

It's not always that fixed. I know of two firms who finally allowed their technical and fundamental research directors to make sell recommendations in a deep down market. Apparently they discovered, belatedly, that they could do business on the downside.

6. *Most recommendations of large houses are published without regard to the technical position of the stock.* That means they neglect the facts as they are in the market at that time.

Believe it or not, several of the Wall Street giants do not have a technical staff. And many of those that do forbid publication, or broad distribution, of technical findings.

Here's what happens:

If the technical picture indicates that XYZ should be bought at 50, they won't tell *you* that. They know that everyone cannot get in at the same time, so that some customers will buy at a much too high price. They do not care about timing a purchase correctly. From past experience, they know that retail clients (you) will purchase approximately 50,000 to 100,000 shares of XYZ in a range from 50 to 57.

They satisfy their own "ethics" by saying, "Well, it will go up to 75 so what the hell is two or five points?"

What happens, of course, is that the favored few—institutions and larger clients—get in at around 50. The public, slow to catch the move, does not start heavy buying until the stock is up to the 57–58 level, just when the Big Boys are ready to sell. Once again, uninformed investors, with the help of friendly brokerage firms, are suckered. And let me assure you they will be, almost every time.

The moral of this story is: If you deal with a large wire house, buy very early or stay out of such institutional-favored stocks.

7. *Incomplete information.* There are times when the giant brokers will recommend an issue only in their Eastern home office and not notify their Southern, Midwest or Western branches. Their justification: "Small clients can time their purchases more advantageously."

Sounds nice, doesn't it? But not when you examine what they are doing. In such situations, it is possible for the firm to generate two commissions:

• From the sell orders from an institution that just *might* have stock to match the buy orders coming in from across the country

• For a regional office that just *might* be ready to start recommending the sale of the stock

As you can see by getting copies of reports, the retail research that large, national firms supply their small clients is seldom worth more than what you pay for it: *nothing*. If you must do business with major brokers, concentrate on their technical studies. At least, those report what really has happened in the market.

Fortunately, not all firms use all of these techniques all of the time. But these are situations of which you should be aware.

CHECK THE BATTING AVERAGES

There's no better way to judge the value of research of a brokerage house than by its batting average: Were the recommendations right more often than they were wrong? When they were right, did they result in worthwhile profits?

Even if a firm has 50 analysts, there's still only one decision maker: the head of research or the president/chairman. In approving research reports, he can be hot or cold, just like anyone else. You want someone who is right the majority of the time.

A handy way to do your own detective work is to get copies of all reports for the past few months or one of those quarterly publications that list recommended stocks by groups.

Six months later, write down the current market prices of these "worthwhile" securities and draw your own conclusions.

AND NOW A COMPLIMENT

I do have a compliment for medium-size, retail-oriented firms, especially those with no more than 15 offices and with strong backgrounds in investment banking. These are organizations where you will find talented RRs who have solid backing from their research departments, both fundamental and technical.

There is a kicker, however. These RRs are making at least $50,000 a year without doing much syndication. Neither they nor their firms want to do business with anyone who has less than $100,000 to invest. They want the big tickets and discourage the small investor.

Why feel like a "poor relation" doing business with a firm like this when there are so many small-to-medium NYSE members that would love to have your business? They do 80 percent of their business with individuals, not institutions.

Many of the talented RRs are men who refused to take the straitjacket approach. They joined the smaller organization in order to practice their profession with imagination and freedom.

My partner is a good example. After serving as head of technical research at one of the top ten Wall Street brokers, he had only one condition when we formed our firm: "I can say and write what I really believe with no holds, regardless of the market climate or client relations."

I agreed and still do. Not only has this arrangement worked well for him, but his freedom of expression has benefited the firm and our clients.

BENEFITS OF SMALLER BROKERAGE FIRMS

Smaller organizations offer specific advantages to small investors:

They must have integrity to survive and prosper. They want your business. They cater to your needs. In most offices, you can walk in and talk to the research people face to face. Or your RR can set up a conference with an analyst and a company officer.

Try getting such personal service with the ivory tower residents of the large brokerage house if you have less than $200,000! Your account gets the same protection, through Securities Investor Protection Corporation as with the biggest members of the NYSE: $50,000. This is the insurance that covers losses when any member firm gets into trouble. In addition, financially strong organizations and small firms that clear through larger brokers carry another $250,000 protection on their own. Your account is protected up to $300,000.

Their overhead is lower. They don't have to support special departments and a chain of offices, many of which are profitable only because of underwritings. In an effort to boost volume, most large houses have become involved in real estate, insurance, tax shelters, bond funds, etc. Those non-brokerage activities build up back-office expenses which produce no profit for you. Without such heavy operational costs, smaller firms can afford to give individual investors personal service.

The RR is paid more: up to 40 percent of the commissions he generates. As a result, the smaller investor is considered important. That's seldom the case with the RR in the giant firm where the take is only 20 percent to 30 percent of total commissions.

CHOOSING YOUR REGISTERED REPRESENTATIVE

A good RR makes investing more understandable, more enjoyable and more profitable. Some financial writers, columnists, commentators and the Wall Street establishment will tell you that to find a competent RR, all you have to do is to walk into a member firm, speak to the manager and let him find a suitable broker for you.

Baloney. Keep your eyes wide open. What are this manager's interests? Since he makes his income based on the commissions generated by his RRs, he is not overly concerned as to what happens to your money. He will probably assign you to the RR who benefits the firm and himself, not you.

In many cases, you will have to do most of the work yourself.

To choose a good RR, follow these guidelines:

1. *A minimum of five years' experience.* Don't let a young broker learn his trade by experimenting on your account. Let him get his training on some-one else's time. His inexperience can cost you a lot of money. No matter how talented a rookie is, let the veteran take the field for the big game. When you are playing to win, there is no substitute for knowledge and know-how.

2. *Earning at least $40,000 a year.* You should always do business with a successful RR even if you have only $5,000 to invest. He will be interested in anyone using margin to buy 500 shares of a stock at 20 because the commission is $175. For writing one ticket and making one phone call, the RR gets from $35 to $70. That commission is the same whether you deal with an inexperienced, low-producing broker who makes only $10,000 a year or with one earning four times as much. Do business with the best in Wall Street: the winners, not the losers.

With a loser, you're more likely to get bad advice, and you run the risk that you'll wake up some morning owning syndicate items that you don't need. Or you will discover that your account is being churned: overtraded for commissions.

The low-income broker will be interested in one thing: making a dollar for himself, not in increasing your capital. The more trades, the higher his income. That's why you should look for a successful broker who doesn't have to churn for his living.

3. *Technically oriented.* I believe that this is what Wall Street is all about. Almost every professional money manager has a technician on his staff. For Wall Street, this is a dramatic change from as short a time as ten years ago. Today technical analysis is accepted and, in many firms, is used more widely than fundamental analysis.

To show you what I mean, let's look at this case history: Honeywell was selling in the mid-40s in March 1976. In early January the stock had broken out at 40 and gone straight up to 56 by mid-February. The next month it dropped back to around 45.

At this point, I called a friend at one of the most respected banking/brokerage firms on Wall Street. I wanted to ask the fundamental reason why HON was down.

Ten, or even three, years ago, I would have received a fundamental answer only. This time, the first words were all technical. He had checked his firm's technician, one of the most knowledgeable researchers on the Street, and had been assured that technically HON was still in an uptrend. There had been no break in the downtrend line, he said.

This points out one of the most difficult areas of technical analysis: interpretation. You must draw your own conclusions. In this case, I disagreed. I felt that the break in the uptrend line, as occurred in April, was a sell signal. Under my strategy the buy signal did not come until June, when there was a breakthrough on the upside at 44.

The point of this comment is that the last thing my friend discussed was fundamental research. He said he had checked various items with company officers and, as far as he could determine, everything was OK. In fact, he told me, he was looking for first-quarter earnings (to be reported on April 19) to be double those of the same period of 1975. Result: I sold HON at 53 when the chart action went down again. The profit was about $7 per share in less than one month.

In my experience, any RR who does not believe in or understand technical analysis is like a fight manager who sends you into the ring against Muhammad Ali with one hand tied behind your back. You're going to get killed!

4. *Understands the "herd instinct" of the institutional investors*—specifically why and how they drive a big stock, like General Motors, up or down 20 percent in a short period (page 61). If the RR is not aware of what makes institutions tick and how to use this power to help his clients make money, move on and look for someone else.

5. *Eats lunch at his desk.* If I were a client, there is no way I would do business with a RR who went out to lunch. A broker who does not work a whole day, from nine to five at a minimum, does not deserve your business!

The stock market is open five days a week, six hours a day, 30 hours a week. If your broker takes a lunch hour, you've missed 15 percent of the trading day. His clients will never get the full picture. If he's not on the job full time, his feel for what's going on will be distorted. Find a broker who will give you full value for your money.

6. *Knows his profession.* There is no sure way to determine how well the RR knows and understands the retail brokerage business. One way to find out is to ask him/her to explain certain techniques outlined in this book. And to ask if there's agreement with the principle of Follow The Leaders.

7. *Has a workable rapport with you.* There are two ways to shatter a good relationship with your broker:

(a) By trying to force an opinion. If he doesn't know, has "bad feelings" or is not sure and wants to ask his research department for guidance, let him. Respect him as a professional. The integrity of a good RR shows in the ability to admit that he cannot know everything. A bad RR (and there are many) will give you an opinion if pressed. He wants to make commissions even though he may really believe that the trade may be unprofitable for you.

(b) By taking too much of the RR's time with unimportant details or for information which is readily available: news of dividends, general opinions on the market, etc.

By doing this, you hurt yourself. Your RR should be busy concentrating on the two most important sources of trading information: the tape and the news ticker.

Plan to make your information-only calls before 9:45 A.M. and after 4 P.M. During the day, ask only about the stocks you own or are thinking of buying: quotes, market action and other items that will take only a minute or two.

Do not be in a hurry to choose your broker. The stock market is a human institution. You are going to have to work with people to make your money grow. If you're not careful and thoughtful, you may select someone who is using you either for his own benefit or as a means to help a large account. Don't be a pawn. Find one of the many good RRs who will like to work for you. This will make life happier and, in the long run, more financially rewarding.

DISCOUNT BROKERS

Wall Street is becoming as competitive as the retail carpet business. You can shop for commissions that will be as much as 70 percent less than you've been paying. With discount brokers it's self-service all the way. These bare bones operations do not provide research recommendations, call attention to new trading opportunities, update charts, monitor breakouts or alert you to sell signals. You have to know what and when you want to trade.

If you follow Blackman Strategy and build your savings to a sizable sum, you should be in a position to get substantial discounts from your present brokerage firm. In Wall Street, volume is the key to profits. An active trader with $25,000 to $50,000 is a far better customer than an inactive investor with $500,000.

Do not be afraid to discuss negotiated rates with your registered representative. If you produce the volume, the broker should reduce your commissions and still provide the data you need. Use the advertisements of discount brokers to get a fair deal.

Advice: Before switching to a discount broker, weigh the dollar savings against the potentially greater profit that should result from help by a knowledgeable, concerned, technically oriented RR.

20.   What the Analysts Really Mean

The language of Wall Street often obfuscates more than it clarifies. This is especially true with research recommendations. Here are some examples of what the analysts say and what I think they really mean.

"We are changing our buy recommendation on XYZ to a hold."
"We would not purchase at this time."
These are manipulative phrases that have no basis in reality. A stock is either a buy or a sell—nothing else. When you read such gobbledygook, it's a good bet that the stocks are part of the brokerage firm's underwriting business and that management does not want to offend the client by an adverse comment. My advice: *Sell* quickly.

"Buy on any breakout including double and triple tops."
This is when new highs are reached two or three times within a relatively short period. See double top of American Broadcasting Companies on page 68) or triple top of Holiday Inns, Inc. on page 195. I buy only on breakouts when the market is very strong and pounding up. Forget about whether the breakout was repetitive. It makes no difference as long as the trend is up.

"Buy into a breakdown."
This is debatable and depends on the individual situation. Trading is an art, not a science. Many times, when I am trading an UP stock, it will drop below the bottom of the channel. Most technicians will avoid purchasing at this time because they believe the uptrend has been broken. I'm more realistic. If the decline is less than 5 percent (two points on a $40 stock) I may take a chance and buy if I am convinced that other factors are favorable: if

it is a high-quality, popular company that has been boosting profits. This is the only type of breakdown I ever consider as a buying possibility.

"The market (stock) was down with profit-taking."

This is the analyst's subtle way of explaining a mistake. He predicted the market, or stock, would go up but the reverse happened. If the trend is really UP, the down fluctuations will be small and meaningless. Smart investors take their profits with a rise, not a decline.

"We are down (up)-rating this stock."

Too often, when this comment is issued by a major brokerage firm, especially one with substantial institutional business, it means that three weeks ago the RRs told their big clients that it was time to: (a) sell if the future report was to be negative; or (b) buy if the analysis is positive. This gave the major investors time to get out or in before the unsuspecting public.

21.   Case History of My Laboratory Account

In January 1975, the market was strong and appeared to be still growing muscle. The way I saw it, the new rally was a humming powerhouse with a chance of being the strongest in years. When the fire's hot, you've got to cook. After five years of bear market blues, I was hungry and ready to go.

I was confident of the money-making value of my strategy and wanted to prove that it could help small investors. This is when I started the Laboratory Account.

As I explained earlier, the idea for this test was the result of questions, misinformation and doubt of the affluent young couple who wanted to start an investment program. I felt that I had to have proof positive of the success of my theories.

I concluded that the best way to make my point was to set up a trade-by-trade case history of how a small investor, using a sensible, diligent investing program, could:

1. Make solid profits and

2. By employing correct selling techniques, keep those gains and use them to improve his/her present life style and assure a worry-free retirement

I proved my point. In six months, Blackman Strategy enabled me to make my capital grow more than ninefold: from $1,569 (with a $4,000 reserve which was used temporarily but promptly replaced) to a total gross value of $18,762.62.

With such limited initial capital, I knew that I had to hunt for the Big Hit. I did not want "miracle" stocks. In my experience they are as profitable as buying mail-order maps to locate sunken treasure. What I needed was a quality, line-drive stock: one that showed the probability of moving up fast because of strong, continuing demand by major institutional investors. With such an UP stock, I could increase my capital and turn my account into a solid leverage tool for further profits. I could not afford to make mistakes. One or two good-sized losses would wreck the account and destroy the effectiveness of the Blackman Strategy.

Determination was a good start, but determination alone is never enough. I would have to check the charts of potentially winning stocks; keep my eyes constantly on the market; maintain discipline enough to take fast, small losses; be ready to move quickly to buy that line-drive stock; and ride it to profits. I had to preserve my investment and make my money grow fast and big. I could not permit hesitation, fuzzy thinking, ignorance or impatience to get in my way.

STARTING THE DRIVE

On January 23, I created the Laboratory Account by depositing 200 shares of Holiday Inns, Inc. The stock was selling at 6⅞, so its value was $1,444.88. To provide for the commissions and to round out the initial investment, I added $124 in cash for an operating base of $1,568.88.

I liked the motel stocks because I thought the "oil crisis" was a big lie and, at current prices, these issues were ultradepressed and ready for an up-swing.

HIA was a quality corporation, rated A− by S&P. Its stock had dropped sharply from over 50. Yet company earnings had fallen only about 25 percent.

The stock market was hot as the Dow moved from 650 to 720 in a few weeks. But I was too anxious. I acted before the overall UP movement was confirmed by the stock chart. Nothing happened with HIA.

It took all my willpower to maintain discipline and to wait. I was ready to make money but the account was running in place. I needed a low-priced line-drive stock.

The groundwork for my first success was laid in early February when the NYSE volume soared to 25 million shares in one day. This was up from an already high 16–18-million-share-a-day level.

On February 12, the opportunity came: Ramada Inns, Inc. (RAM) broke out. This stock was rated fourth in quality in the motel group, but everything was promising. This was an UP stock in an UP group in an UP market. When such a situation develops, I don't wait. I move.

I sold the 200 shares of HIA for a small profit and bought 4000 shares of RAM at the 3¼ to 3½ level. Then I day-traded (bought and sold in the same day) and, within two days, sold out at 4 to 4¼. My profit was $1,371, nearly doubling my investment.

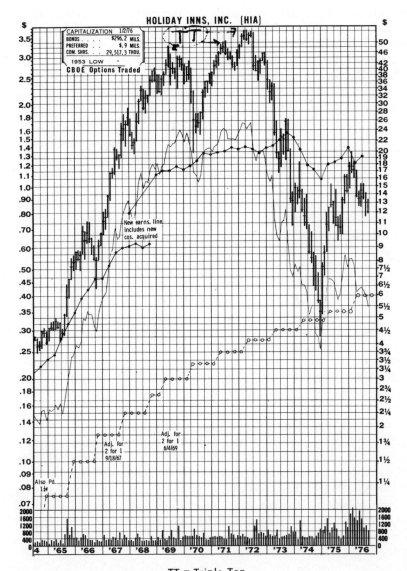

TT = Triple Top

Note: During this period, I did put up an additional, $4,211 to meet margin requirements and to buy 200 shares of Fisher Scientific. I withdrew this immediately after the RAM sale. I did this sort of thing later, on several other fast trades but always returned this temporary support in order not to distort the real dollar results of the Lab Account. I justify this action because from experience I know that my clients seldom use full margin and thus maintain reserve buying power for just such profit opportunities.

Having the patience to wait for a good stock that would go straight up by 20 percent without a correction and concentrating my capital had paid off. The account started to click. My techniques were working.

I took a small, fast loss of $99 in Fisher. Here again, I was too early. The chart looked good but there was no positive follow-up confirmation, so I sold quickly. Subsequently Fisher doubled in value but I didn't care. I knew I had a sound system. I was making money and had no time to cry about what might have been. Second-guessing will dull your strategy, and with small capital you cannot afford any form of carelessness. If your projections do not come true quickly, sell.

Now I could look for a Big Hit. While waiting, I traded some home-building stocks when their charts looked good. On March 6, RAM looked good again. The chart showed an UP drive with heavy volume. I bought 500 shares at 4⅛ and, because I believe in buying UP (staying with a profitable move), I acquired 1,000 more shares at 4¼. It's a satisfactory feeling to know that you are putting your money into a rising situation. You're paying higher prices but you have the cushion of an earlier profit. And you are obeying that important rule of concentration.

The next day, RAM went to 5¼, up 20 percent plus—a welcome gain of $799.92. I sold to protect my profits and because I felt that the market was getting a bit toppy and due for a correction. As it turned out, I acted too soon. RAM continued up.

In a slow UP market, a 20 percent jump can take from two weeks to three months. In this hot market, it took two days. My techniques were working well with the strong market. RAM went to 5¾ but I remembered that old saying, "Bulls make money; bears make money; but hogs don't."

Actually, it's much better to sell too soon. When a stock is still going up, you are assured that you'll find a buyer quickly. You have liquidity. If you have no buyer, you're stuck unless you accept a lower price. Buyers are always there when the market is going up. They evaporate when the market is going down.

To emphasize this point, let me jump forward one year. In May 1976, I bought Bucyrus-Erie (BY) for my own account. This was rated B+, had strong institutional ownership and was involved in the burgeoning fields of

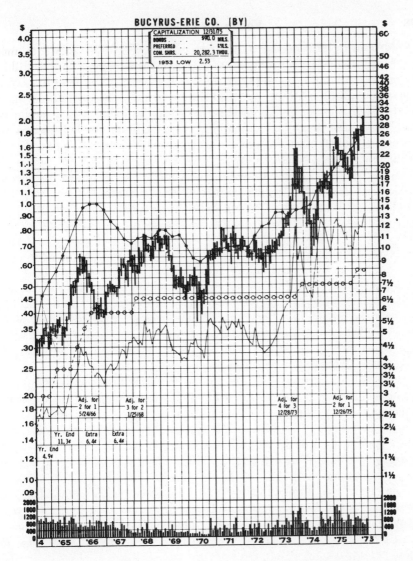

coal mining and environmental controls. The chart showed that, after a temporary dip, the stock had moved to an all-time high and was driving UP again.

I started buying at 27 and filled my position at 27½, just before a 100,000-share day triggered another new high.

The next day, I did not like the looks of the market, especially when BY opened at 28⅛ with only 700 shares. I put in my 1,000 shares to sell at market. That morning, the Dow was down three points and fell six for the day. My prices, on my 1,000 shares, were 100 at 27⅛, 100 at 27⅝ and 800 at 27½. This was just before the lack of interest that dropped the stock to 27. There was no liquidity: trading of only 3,100 shares including my 1,000.

This proved to me how important it is to sell into strength in an UP market. Here was an institutional stock with a 30 million-share capitalization. It had made a major breakthrough; yet, when the market went down, the buyers disappeared. By being willing to sell for a small, quick profit, I saved myself from a substantial loss.

Now let's get back to the Laboratory Account. In early March 1975, when I sold Ramada Inn stock, I felt the market was nearing a top. On March 11, I backed up this feeling by shorting 200 shares of Automatic Data at 46. The market came in (went down) so I covered at 43½ for a small, quick profit of $196.

When the market correction ended, I felt that the market was ready to go up again so I got out my hunting gear and looked for the next Big Hit. It was a long search. I continued to trade but couldn't make important money. I was running in place through the month of April. It was irritating not to be able to make money in a hot market. Time became a factor. I figured the market would go big until the middle of July because usually markets run well for six months when the capital-gains profit-takers move in. This bull market had started in January.

I was still exercising tight discipline, being patient, and using solid trading techniques. But I knew that I had only two months left in the strong market move. I didn't panic but bore down even harder in my search.

In the first weekend in May, while working on my technical and fundamental studies, I noticed that Gulf & Western Industries (GW) was trying to break out of a two-year V formation. The stock was hovering in the low 30s.

There were two strong factors: (1) GW was one of the quality conglomerates, rated A— by S&P; (2) the V formation (see long-term chart herewith) is one of the most powerful signals in chart reading. This could be an UP stock in an UP group even though the overall market was still indefinite.

After checking all three charts, I realized that if GW could go to 36, it could move to 44 for that 20 percent gain. This was evident from channels drawn across the tops and bottoms. This formed a very clear path.

I felt that the institutional chartists saw this possibility. To check my projections, I reviewed the fundamentals. G&W was earning $8.00 a share, up from $5.50 the preceding year. One of its divisions was Paramount Pictures, which had produced *The Godfather*. This was a huge success, raking in millions of dollars. Just as in the 1930s, when the movie business zoomed as an escape from the misery of the depression, so Hollywood was getting fat from the recession of the early 1970s.

I also discovered that other G&W divisions, primarily manufacturing, were growing at better than the 20 percent-a-year rate. The statistics were mouth-watering. The short-term technical position looked just as tasty—a strong uptrend. In late May 1975, the stock started to move up from 36, which was at the bottom of the channel.

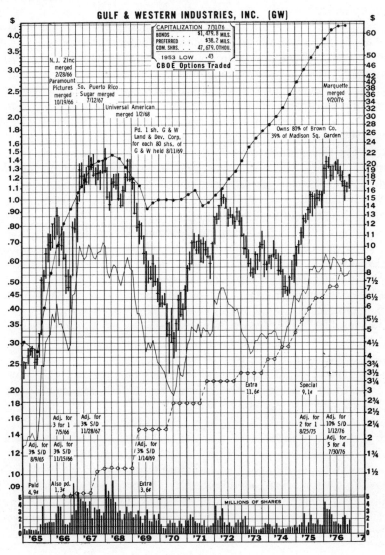

GULF & WESTERN INDUSTRIES, INC. (GW)

The overall market looked great, so I checked other conglomerates such as ITT, Litton and Textron. Most of them were in strong uptrends, too.

I had ten weeks to go on my timetable. GW looked like my next Big Hit. The market was UP, the conglomerate group was UP and GW was an UP stock, the strongest in the group. The block trades (those involving over 5,000 shares) were all on uptick (at ever higher prices). Clearly there were many more buyers than sellers as the institutions were starting to pile into this group and stock.

To be absolutely sure, I went back to the fundamentals again. I saw that GW had 14 million common shares plus 7 million warrants. These were convertible at $53 and expired in January 1978. With one warrant plus $53, you could buy one share of common stock.

Here was a chance for leverage. Since warrants sell at much lower prices than do related stocks, the same dollar investment can buy more warrants. With GW, the warrants were selling at about 5 when the stock was at 34. Usually, warrants move parallel to their stocks so their percentage gain is greater when there's an UP move.

Better yet, these warrants were traded on the NYSE, so they could be bought on margin (not generally available with warrants traded elsewhere). Everything looked great. With such a large capitalization, there would be great liquidity. I could beat the institutions in and out.

The more I studied the situation, the more certain I became that GW could be a genuine line-drive stock with which I could score a double-barreled hit: big gains with a small investment. I figured that the warrants could go to 10 (or more) if the stock hit 44.

On Monday morning, May 5, when GW common was at 34, I started to buy the warrants at around 5. The Dow Average took a 40-point dive in the next two weeks but GW held well: between a high of 36½ and a low of 33½. More important, it never broke the uptrend line on the chart.

The warrants traded to a high of 5¼ and a low of 4⅝. I started buying: 1,500 at 5, 500 at 4¾ on May 19 and 500 at 4⅞ on June 2nd: 2,500 all told. To do this I had to call on my reserve and use margin. My clients were also loaded with both the stock and the warrants.

On June 1, GW stock hit a new high, going through 37 and closing at 37½. This is always great to see. I felt that this was *it* and my Laboratory Account was almost home.

However, a funny thing happened before I could go to the bank with my profits: the stock market halted and started to go down. I decided to hold my position as long as the stock did not break down through the uptrend line. I felt that any correction would be mild. It was: the Dow stopped at 810, down from 840. At the same time, GW stock held firm between 38 and 36.

After the July 4th holiday, there was one more Roman candle still waiting to explode. GW stock took off and became a sure line-driver. In seven days, it shot from 37 to 44 with daily volume of over 100,000 shares. It was on the Most Active list, thereby drawing more players. The red-hot tape action attracted more retail accounts and the warrants burned the tape, also on the Most Active list with a jump to over 9. This was the Big Hit I'd been waiting for.

On Monday, July 14, the market indexes, which I keep up-to-date daily, gave a general sell signal. This is an inviolable signal under Blackman Strategy.

This red light was reinforced by other sell signals by GW stock:

• At 43, it reached the top of its uptrend channel, moved up about a point, then dropped back. The UP drive had been broken

• The volume was the heaviest it had been since April

• The overall market had been rising for six months, indicating that a top, and sell-off, was due

Now I had four reasons to sell. Any *one* of these was a strong signal; the combination had to be obeyed.

The market was still hot, but I had a large position to liquidate. For once, time was on my side. I knew that it would take the committee-run institutions two or three days to act, and that, since retail clients of the superlarge brokerage firms would get the news late, I could get out early and easily.

On July 15 I started selling GW warrants and received an average price between 9¼ and 9⅜. A few days later, some of my die-hard clients did a fraction better and sold at 9½. They were lucky, not smart.

Now the money was in the Lab Account at the bank. I was out of the market for the time being. The profit on the 2,500 warrants, after all commissions and costs, was $10,313!

A few days later I saw a chance for a quick profit and bought and sold 2,000 GW warrants the same day for a gain of $760. And, as a final gesture, I made another $169 with a fast buy and sell of 400 shares of MCA.

In six months the Laboratory Account had made a gross of $18,762.62. If I had paid full commissions at the old, fixed 100 percent rate charged by NYSE firms prior to May 1975, the net profits would have been $14,816.79— all on an original investment of $1,568.88 (plus the temporary use of the reserve fund)—in about six months.

As this case history shows, I didn't make money and keep it through astrology, "expert" advice or gambling. I worked hard, followed Blackman Strategy and disciplined myself to act according to my rules. You can do the same if you pick an UP stock in an UP group in an UP market and follow the leaders by watching the chart signals.

BLACKMAN LABORATORY ACCOUNT
1975

No. of Shares	Security	Date of Purchase	Date of Sale	Cost	Proceeds	S/T Profit (Loss)	Deposits—	Date	With-drawals—	Date
200	Holiday Inns Inc.	1/24	2/20	1,444.88	1,700.36	255.48	+ 124.00	1/17		
200	Fisher Scientific Co.	2/05	2/24	1,498.28	1,399.13	(99.15)	+4,211.00	2/18	−4,211.00	2/21
500	Ramada Inns Inc.	2/12	2/13	1,697.91	1,930.46	232.55				
1500	Ramada Inns Inc.	2/13	2/13	5,410.40	5,791.38	380.98				
500	Ramada Inns Inc.	2/13	2/14	1,803.46	2,065.49	251.03				
1500	Ramada Inns Inc.	2/13	2/14	5,410.41	5,976.17	565.76				
500	Ramada Inns Inc.	2/13	2/20	1,803.48	1,976.73	173.25				
300	Travelers Corp.	2/25	3/04	6,919.33	7,018.62	99.29				
1500	Ramada Inns Inc.	3/06	3/07	6,509.74	7,309.46	799.72	+ 116.00	3/03		
200	Auto. Data Proc. (Short Sale)	3/12	3/11	8,846.45	9,042.49	196.04				
1000	Skyline Corp.	3/14	3/14	17,559.40	18,033.72	474.32				
600	Champion Home Bldrs.	3/14	3/17	2,339.23	2,601.15	261.92				
1000	Elixir Industries	3/14	3/17	5,418.56	5,575.30	156.74	+ 163.00	3/18		
200	Petrie Stores Corp.	3/26	3/31	10,986.46	11,183.31	196.85	+3,726.00	3/21		
200	New England Nuclear	4/04	4/29	5,040.73	5,342.52	301.79				
500	Holiday Inns Inc.	4/11	5/01	5,523.20	6,270.49	747.29				
5 calls	Pfizer Inc. April 35	4/16	4/16	203.25	360.65	157.40				
5000	AT&T Wts.	4/30	5/01	942.76	1,053.72	110.96			−3,800.00	3/26
1500	Gulf & Western Wts.	5/05	7/15	7,650.00	13,567.22	5,917.22	+1,600.00	5/06		
5 calls	Gulf & Western Ind. July 35	5/07	5/07	1,562.50	1,724.96	162.46				
500	Browning-Ferris Ind.	5/08	5/08	3,065.00	3,328.68	263.68				
5 calls	Gulf & Western Ind. July 35	5/08	5/15	1,775.00	1,787.46	12.46	+1,000.00	5/23		
500	Gulf & Western Wts.	5/19	7/16	2,410.00	4,642.41	2,232.41				

5 calls	Gulf & Western Ind. July 35	5/23	7/01	1,462.50	1,599.96	137.46	− 400.00	7/03
500	Gulf & Western Wts.	6/02	7/16	2,477.50	4,642.40	2,164.90	−1,700.00	7/16
700	Seaboard World Air.	6/05	6/24	4,249.00	4,324.16	75.16		
200	Rite Aid Corp.	6/19	6/30	2,426.00	2,764.19	338.19	+ 596.00	6/26
300	Castle & Cooke Inc.	6/25	7/15	5,148.00	5,008.77	(139.23)		
100	Pittsburgh-DesMoines	7/08	7/09	2,032.50	2,688.44	655.94		
100	Castle & Cooke Inc.	7/08	7/15	1,719.00	1,669.59	(49.41)		
5 calls	Northwest Airlines October 20	7/08	7/16	1,243.75	1,724.96	481.21		
100	Pittsburgh-DesMoines	7/09	7/09	2,419.00	2,578.44	159.44		
100	Pittsburgh-DesMoines	7/09	7/09	2,419.00	2,578.44	159.44		
2000	Gulf & Western Wts.	7/22	7/22	16,120.00	16,879.66	759.66		
400	MCA Inc.	7/24	(300) 7/24 (100) 7/25	29,000.00	29,169.41	169.41		

S/T Profit	$19,050.41
S/T Loss	−287.79
TOTAL S/T Profit	18,762.62

Suggested Reading

For further information on technical analysis and charts, here's a list of books to buy or to read at your local library. Although I do not agree with some of the theories and many of the conclusions, nevertheless you may find some interesting and, hopefully, worthwhile information.

Technical Analysis of Stock Trends by Robert D. Edwards and John Magee. John Magee Associates, Springfield, Mass.

Investing for Profit with Technical Analysis of Stock Market Cycles by William C. Garrett. Prentice-Hall.

Strategy of Daily Stock Market Timing for Maximum Profit by Joseph E. Granville. Prentice-Hall.

Market Timing for Maximum Profits by Joseph E. Granville. Prentice-Hall.

Stock Market Behavior: The Technical Approach to Understanding Wall Street by Harvey A. Krow. Random House.

Financial Analyst's Handbook by Sumner N. Levine. Dow Jones-Irwin.

The Battle for Investment Survival by Gerald M. Loeb. Simon and Schuster.

The Battle for Stock Market Profits by Gerald M. Loeb. Simon and Schuster.

Money and Stock Market Prices by Beryl W. Sprinkel. Dow Jones-Irwin.

Glossary

ADVISORY SERVICES: Independent purveyors of stock market advice who have yet to make enough money from their own recommendations to retire.

AMERICAN STOCK EXCHANGE (AMEX): Where the stocks of smaller and less seasoned corporations are traded. In past boom markets, this is where speculators found action. One sign of a stock market top is when prices and volume on this exchange become too frantic.

ANALYSTS: Statisticians who arrange and rearrange figures given to them by those who really know what's happening. They are not famous for knowing when to get out of a deteriorating situation.

AVERAGING:
    Up: Adding to an original stock position as it goes up. Considered sound and aggressive strategy.
    Down: Continuing to buy as the price declines. A fine way to get bagged permanently in the wrong stock. It is done only by those who need a psychological boost for their egos.

BAGGED: When you are stuck with a loss, paper or real.

BANKING/BROKERAGE FIRM: Compared to large wire houses, these are smaller in size, but often bigger in capital. The quality of their advice is superior to most recommendations available in Wall Street.

BARGAIN HUNTERS: Those hardy, but stupid, souls who buy on bad news.

BEAR MARKET: This is a declining market. It's a good time to sell short or stay out of stocks. Most people, especially the more bullish "experts," don't recognize it until it's almost over.

BOARDROOM SITTER: Someone who spends many hours sitting in a brokerage office watching the stock tape and trading his securities. Generally these are people who are losers or show minor profits.

BOOK: This refers to the specialist's book containing a listing of all limit orders—that is, those which are to be executed when the stock hits a predetermined price.

BOTTOM: This is an area which is apparent only through hindsight. In a bear market it's the place where most people are convinced that things will get worse. This is the hardest to pick, but most profitable, point at which to buy stocks.

BULL MARKET: This is when the prices of stocks are going up. It is the time to be fully invested, to use your resources to the best advantage. Often, conditions may not appear to be bullish but the stock market anticipates. A good sign of a coming rise is the presence of many skeptics.

BUYING UP: This is adding to a winning decision by purchasing additional stock as its price rises. A higher price confirms the rightness of the original buy decision.

BUYING DOWN: This is almost always a losing practice. It ignores the fact that a bad decision was made originally, and, regardless of the excuse, the buy was wrong.

CALL OPTIONS: Generally speaking, options give the buyer, or holder, the right to acquire a form of property—in this case, stocks—within a specified future time period at a specific price. If not exercised within the specified time, the option expires worthless. The market value of the option will fluctuate along with changes in the price of the related stock and the life of the call. You can buy or sell calls, or you can use a combination in hedging. To the unsophisticated, buying calls appears to be a cheap way to speculate in high-priced stocks. Unfortunately, buyers of calls lose in 90 percent of their ventures. This is a total loss of the capital employed.

Hedging (also called *Spreading*) is a form of arbitrage: buying one security and selling, or selling short, another. It may be profitable or result in small losses but, in most cases, it is a complex operation that requires experience and detailed projections. Commissions reduce profits for amateur investors.

CALL SHEET: This is a sales tool used by the large brokerage firms. It will list the names, addresses, and phone numbers of prospective buyers and the results, if any, of all telephone calls made by the registered representative on a particular day or evening.

CAPITAL GAINS: For most investors, this is an excuse for being too greedy and holding a profitable position too long—over nine months. It's also an excuse for delaying the making of a difficult sell decision.

CHANNEL: The trading range for a stock as shown on a chart. The channel is formed by parallel lines that slant upward in bullish situations, downward in bearish movements. This is one of the chief tools of the technician, who uses the boundaries set by the parallel lines as a guide in buy and sell decisions. The violation (breakthrough) of the channel line, or trendline, is a major signal: bullish when the break is up, bearish when the violation is down. This applies to an individual stock or, when used wtih a major stock average, to the market as a whole.

CHART: A picture of a particular stock, industry group or market average. Charts are the primary tool of the stock market technician. Their interpretation is an art, not a science, and can lead to problems. Even experienced chartists disagree on the meaning of identical formations. The key factor, always, is the use of trend-lines which show the direction of the stock-price movement. Almost everyone agrees with what an UP stock is, but certain technicians like to pick special patterns—bottoms, reversals, head & shoulders, etc.—to be smart. The question to ask every technical analyst is: "Was there a profit or loss at the end of the year with your system?"

CHART BREAK: This occurs when the price of a stock moves through a level that previously has not been violated. It can occur on the upside or downside. When it does take place, it will command your attention and usually will require a decision to buy or to sell.

CHART SERVICES: These are some of the companies that publish and sell stock charts and other market indicators. The charts are constructed for short and long term: i.e., daily, weekly, monthly, yearly or for 10 and 12 years. Some services include professional interpretations of the charts. Among these services are:

Trendline, Inc., 345 Hudson Street, New York, N.Y. 10014
Daily Basis Stock Charts (weekly)   Year $280*
Current Market Perspectives (monthly)   Year 84*
OTC Chart Manual (bi-monthly)   Year 75*
   * plus postage
Securities Research Company, 208 Newbury Street, Boston, Mass. 02116
3 Trend Security Charts (monthly)   Year $59
Wall Charts (quarterly)   Year 12
3 Trend Cycli-Graphs—12 years (quarterly) Year 37
   Plus postage for first class delivery
R. W. Mansfield Co., 26 Journal Square, Jersey City, N.J. 07306
For NYSE, AMEX and OTC
For one service (monthly)   Year $130*
       (every other week)   Year 240*
       (weekly)   Year 450
                        * plus postage
Chartcraft, Inc., One West Avenue, Larchmont, N.Y. 10538
NYSE & AMEX (weekly)   Year $180
        (monthly)   Year 192

CHARTIST: Sometimes referred to as a "technician," a "tea leaf reader" or "the one with all the lines going every which way." A chartist is an individual who makes market decisions based on his reading of charts and other technical indicators.

CHURN: Unethical trading of a customer's account solely for the broker's commissions.

COMMISSION: The transaction cost of trading securities. Usually, the percentage of the value involved is smaller as the order gets larger.

CONGLOMERATES: These are large companies whose growth was accomplished by the acquisition of many smaller, unrelated businesses and whose present management is directed by a headquarters group. Their structure is different from vertically integrated corporations where acquisitions involve companies in related aspects of the same industry. Shares of conglomerates carry low price/earnings ratios in the stock market because the underlying operations are difficult to analyze. These firms often carry large debt, and usually have a capitalization with the potential of substantial dilution of the common stock.

CONCENTRATION CONCEPT: Putting a high proportion of one's market funds in relatively few stocks (or even one). My rule of thumb for stock market holdings: for $25,000 capital, one stock; up to $50,000, two stocks; $100,000, a maximum of four issues.

CONSOLIDATION: This usually occurs after a stock has had a sharp move, either up or down. It is a period of digestion characterized by a relatively flat movement and light volume. It's a bad time for investors because profits, if any, are meager. You should be in cash in such periods.

CORRECTION: This usually refers to a reversal from the major trend. It implies that what went before was wrong—which of course may not be so. Some brokers prefer using this term to being candid and saying that the market is moving down. It's my experience that the word "correction" is used mainly by people who do not understand what the hell is happening.

CYCLICAL: This definition can be applied to overall market patterns as well as to individual company patterns. It refers to the up and down swings of corporate/industry sales and earnings: such swings are characteristic of steel, aluminum, construction, transportation and machinery companies.

DAY TRADE: Buying and selling (or short selling and covering) on the same day in hopes of a quick profit. This technique uses a minimal amount of margin but is difficult to complete successfully.

DECLINING: This is another word for "down." It is applicable to both markets and stocks. See STOCK: *declining*.

DISCIPLINE: This requires that the investor avoid natural emotional reactions and that he adhere to the principles outlined in this book.

DISCRETIONARY ACCOUNT: A type of account that gives the broker legal authority to make buy and sell decisions for the customer. Such an arrangement requires good rapport and a clear understanding of risks and objectives. In some cases, overtrading may crop up, but usually such accounts can be made to work. Although some larger firms will not accept such accounts, they can be true tests of what a broker can accomplish when given freedom and opportunity. If your discretionary account drops 15 percent, close it and find a new broker.

DISTRIBUTION CENTERS: This is a term used to describe retail offices of large brokerage firms. These branches are used as supermarkets to sell underwritings of securities.

DIVERSIFICATION: The opposite of concentration. A defensive type of investment strategy. It admits a certain lack of knowledge and insight and relies on the theory of "safety in numbers." A disastrous investing system for those who want to make substantial gains in the stock market.

DIVIDENDS: These are payments to shareholders from a company's earnings. They are akin to the interest on a savings account but are not guaranteed. Of no concern to traders.

DOW JONES AVERAGES: The best known of all stock market indicators. They consist of three separate averages made up of leading stocks: industrials (30); transportation (20); and utilities (15). At certain times, any or all of the averages can be misleading and create false impressions regarding market strength or weakness because of the limited number of issues involved. Still, they are the best benchmarks for what's happening in Wall Street. Use them.

DOWNSIDE: A technical term used to indicate possible degree of risk for a stock (or the market). It is determined by support levels shown on charts.

DOWNTREND: Opposite of uptrend. See CHANNELS.

EARNINGS FORECAST: A weekly publication that reports projected earnings of major corporations. It is available for $200 a year from Standard & Poor's, 345 Hudson Street, New York, N.Y. 10014.

FAST, SMALL LOSS: This is the best kind to take. Traders limit losses by selling when: (1) a stock falls one or two points; (2) the decline is equivalent to the cost of a round-trip commission; (3) the drop is a preset percentage of the cost price, usually from 3% to 10%.

FUNDAMENTAL RESEARCH: This refers to analysis based on the financial facts and reported figures relating to the company and its industry. Basic factors include the rate of growth of sales and earnings, the balance sheet and income statement and the return on stockholders' equity for the past five to ten years. These data are often supplemented by visits with corporate management, inspection of company properties, conversations with competitors and studies of industry statistics.

Although this research may be done in a competent manner, conclusions can be misapplied if the timing element is ignored. The stock market is not so interested in past and present performance as it is in projections of the future. Too many fundamentalists ignore the importance of timing in the belief that investors will eventually give proper recognition to good fundamentals. This may be true when you own investments with good names and backgrounds, but there are no profits until such values are recognized and result in higher stock prices.

HERD INSTINCT: The tendency of large investors to act alike in both buying and selling stocks. Such group action can cause exaggerated and volatile moves—up and down. If enough institutions take the same side of the market, there can be a stampede, with either a high gain or a rapid loss.

Large institutions do not want highly individualistic or overly adventuresome portfolio managers. They prefer to play the game conventionally and conservatively. That's why there tends to be a certain sameness in their approach to securities. You must understand this herd instinct to survive and prosper in the world of the behemoths.

HOLD: This is one of the most abused words on Wall Street. Occasionally those who use it actually mean "Hang on." More often it is a euphemism for "sell." The stock has not performed as expected and the people who recommended purchase are unwilling to adjust their error.

HOLD CASH: A wise plan of action in down markets. This assures the ability to commit money quickly if conditions warrant.

INSTITUTIONAL STOCKS: These are the types of equities that the large investors prefer to own. They are shares of quality corporations—those rated B+ or higher in Standard & Poor's Stock Guide. Generally these companies have capitalization of 5 million shares, of which 300,000 are owned by at least ten institutions.

INSTITUTIONS: Large organizations investing other people's money: e.g., mutual funds, pension plans, insurance companies, banks, foundations, college endowment funds, etc.

INVOLUNTARY INVESTOR: This is the unfortunate individual who buys for a quick profit, sees the stock go down, doesn't sell, and holds on regardless of the extent of the loss.

LINE-DRIVE STOCK: This is the looked-for stock that goes straight up 20% or more without a significant correction.

LIQUIDATE: The important, and usually wise, decision to sell all stocks to go into cash and wait for new opportunities.

LONDON AVERAGE: This is the *London Financial Times* Index of the action of a select list of stocks traded on the London Stock Exchange. It is a tool that smart professionals use as an indicator of the direction of the New York market.

LONG: Owning stock.

MARGIN: Using borrowed money to buy securities. It is usually expressed as a percentage of the funds the buyer must put up. In January 1974 the margin was reduced from 65% to 50% by the Federal Reserve Board.

MUTUAL FUNDS: These are investment companies whose shares are sold to and bought from the public at net asset value. The money is invested by the professional managers in a diversified portfolio of stocks and/or bonds. The fund pays no taxes if 90% of the income is distributed to shareholders. The portfolios are structured to meet different investment objectives: growth, income, balance, etc. In recent years the results of mutual fund investments have not been so good as those of many knowledgeable investors.

NEW YORK STOCK EXCHANGE (NYSE): This grandaddy of American stock exchange (formed in 1792) trades the shares of most large corporations. It's an auction market where prices are set by open bidding. Despite the development of a consolidated tape (showing transactions on all American stock exchanges) and the SEC's attempt to downgrade its role, the Big Board accounts for 85% of all trading of shares of 1,600+ listed companies.

NEWS TICKER: A general term referring to the teletype and electronic display devices used by Dow Jones and Reuters News Services to provide a constant flow of financial/business news to brokerage offices. The ticker can be a major influence on stock prices. Some boardroom sitters "trade off the ticker"—on the basis of the news. This is not recommended because: (1) important financial news has already been discounted by major investors; (2) usually, your initial gut reaction is wrong in translating news into market action.

NO-NEWS RALLY: A rally generated by the internal forces of the marketplace itself. It happens without the spark of any specific news item, so is the best type of rally to buy into.

NOT HELD TO BUY OR SELL: This is an order that gives the floor broker (the firm's representative in the trading area of the exchange), discretion in execution of an order. A straight buy order will be relayed directly to the stock specialist. With a not held to buy order, you are trusting the floor broker's judgment to get a better price. When a stock is selling at 50, a straight buy order would be executed at the price, or within ⅛ point. With a NHTB order, it might be completed at 49¾ or lower. But there is also the chance that the stock will move up and you will have to pay 50½ or higher. This technique is worthwhile only when dealing with 500 or more shares.

ODD LOT: A purchase or sale of less than 100 shares of stock.

OPTIONS: *See* CALL OPTIONS.

OVER-THE-COUNTER (OTC): This describes the market where shares of companies not listed on stock exchanges are traded. A few are large corporations such as banks and insurance companies, but most are small, unseasoned, closely controlled firms. This is a dealer market in that the broker/dealer sells from, and buys for, his own inventory. He may acquire the shares from another dealer and resell them at a price to include his markup. Or he may buy the stock and hold it for price appreciation. Under the regulations of the National Association of Securities Dealers (NASD), the broker must get three quotations on each customer's buy order. Markups are regulated by the SEC and NASD.

PAPER LOSS: There is no such thing. The term is merely a salve to the ego. A loss is a loss. Whether or not the trader wishes to sell and accept the fact that the deal was unprofitable depends on how well he is disciplined.

PORTFOLIO: The sum total of all investments, whatever they may be.

PORTFOLIO MANAGER: A professional who directs investments for an institution. The position, one of the more prestigious and lucrative positions in the financial field, usually requires a background in fundamental analysis.

RALLY: An upward move in the market and/or individual stocks from a down or quiet market. Generally the reason for the rise will not be apparent at the time, and often is referred to as "technical." See *no-news rally*.

RATE OF GROWTH: This is the percentage of increase in corporate earnings over a number of years: for example, in the past five years XYZ's profits per share have been $.20, $.30, $.45, $.67 and $1.00. Since each year's earnings were 50% higher than those of the previous year, the rate of earnings growth is 50%. This is the single most important fundamental factor influencing a stock's movement. Continually stronger earnings growth implies future price appreciation and higher dividend payouts. Usually the current stock price reflects anticipated profits and higher future dividends.

REGISTERED REPRESENTATIVE (RR): This is the official designation of a broker who is legally authorized to deal in securities. The RR may also be a source of useful investment and trading information and timely market advice.

REGISTRATION: A corporation is said to be in registration when some type of securities offering is pending. At such a time, the SEC is examining the prospectus and the underwriter is forming a marketing syndicate. For a brief period, usually 40 days, both before and after the stock is sold, no one in the corporation or employed by a firm that is a member of the syndicate may give out projections or opinions regarding that issue. The prospectus is supposed to provide full factual data to enable the investor to formulate an opinion of the merits of the issue.

REPORTS: These written documents can contain useful information as compiled by analysts at brokerage firms and investment advisory services. Unfortunately they are seldom available to individual investors until after someone, somewhere, has already acted. Therefore, by the time you get the report, the market price of the stock probably already reflects (or has discounted) the data. Insiders have friends, relatives, or business associates who somehow release the information early. You must learn to accept the fact that there are such leaks, lest you put too much reliance on what is really "old" news.

RESEARCH WIRE: This is a separate communications system that large brokerage firms use to provide their registered representatives with research information. Usually such wires are operating all day long with a large volume of so-called pertinent data.

RETAIL CLIENTS: These are the much maligned individual investors who, at large brokerage firms, receive far less attention than do institutional customers. Many of these "little guys" show more common sense and achieve greater success in the stock market than do the professional money managers.

RETAIL FIRMS: These are brokers who specialize in handling smaller individual clients and seldom seek out large institutional business.

ROUND LOT: This is a Wall Street term to describe the buying or selling of 100 shares of stock. This is the opposite of *Odd lot*, which means transactions of fewer than 100 shares.

SEC: Securities and Exchange Commission, an agency of the federal government set up to police and regulate brokers, stock exchanges, public trading of securities, and financial reports and accounting of publicly owned corporations.

SCALE: Buying or selling over a period of time at a succession of slightly different prices: i.e., at 10, 12, 11 and 9. An institution will instruct a broker to average purchases or sales as best he can. In such scale buying, volume is always a restrictive factor.

SECURITIES: This is a general term used to describe printed certificates denoting ownership of stocks (preferred and common); bonds (of governments and corporations); instruments (notes and bills); shares of mutual funds; convertible issues, etc.

SELL AT THE MARKET: This means to accept the best available price for the stock. This is the fastest way to get out of a position. Once the decision to sell has been made, and particularly in a declining market, sell at the market. Those who delay and haggle over ⅛ point may find they've missed out and will have to accept a much lower price.

SELL SIGNAL, GENERAL TECHNICAL: See the rules in Chapter XIV.

SELL SIGNAL, INDIVIDUAL: This is a technical term meaning that the charts of an individual stock show clearly the necessity of selling. Usually, there will be a break in the uptrend line or channel indicating that the up momentum has ceased.

SELLS: The easiest way for a broker to recommend a sale is to say "Sell." Investors should understand that Wall Street has other ways of recommending "Sell":

(1) An analyst will say he likes a stock but thinks that it will "underperform" the market;

(2) The use of the word "hold." When a research report or broker's recommendation switches a stock from a "buy" to a "hold" list, he now thinks the stock has moved up too much to buy, and in effect is saying that you are on your own to decide when to sell. A "hold" recommendation takes the broker off the hook and puts the responsibility on the customer.

SEVENTY-TWO, RULE OF: This states that by dividing the rate of interest into 72, your answer will be the number of years it takes your money to double when earning that rate of return: for instance, at 6%, your savings will double in 12 years (72 ÷ 6 = 12).

SHORT: You sell short when you expect prices to drop. You do not own the stock but use borrowed shares as arranged by your broker. Thus, a bearish investor sells 100 shares of a stock at 50. He waits for the stock to drop to, say, 40, then buys 100 shares to cover his short position. The purchased stock is delivered to the original lender. The investor chalks up a 10-point ($1,000) profit.

On the other hand, if the stock goes up and the short seller decides to cover at 60, he has a 10-point ($1,000) loss. These figures do not include deductions for commissions and premiums (for hard-to-borrow stock) and for dividends paid to the stock owner.

SIDEWAYS MARKET: This exists in name only. Actually, it's a down market, because investors are not making money.

SPECIALISTS: These are exchange members who work on the floor of the stock exchange and are responsible for making markets in individual stocks. They are a key element in the auction market. Specialists are entrepreneurs who use their own capital to maintain an orderly market in the stocks that they handle by assignment from the exchange. They must have a keen market sense, iron nerves and large amounts of capital. For a fee, they execute public orders left with them by brokers. They assure liquidity by making bids and offers for their own accounts.

The performance of all specialists is evaluated frequently by the exchange and the SEC. All operations must meet stringent rules and guidelines, all designed to protect the public. Depending on current market conditions, they can profit handsomely or lose substantially.

SPLIT: Stock splits are made by corporations in order to lower the price of their shares and provide wider distribution and greater liquidity. By itself a stock split changes nothing: 1,000,000 shares at $50 equals $50,000,000 market value. When split 2 for 1, the 2,000,000 shares, now at $25, still have $50,000,000 market value. Sometimes a stock split will be accompanied by a dividend increase.

News of a split may push up the price of a stock temporarily but this is usually followed by a long period of selling, which may cancel out the stock's rise. It is unwise to buy a stock once a split announcement has been made because the event has already been discounted and there is little chance of a substantial gain.

STAMPEDE: See HERD INSTINCT.

STANDARD & POOR'S: This is a leading supplier of statistical/financial information. Through various published reports and services S&P supplies data on thousands of public corporations, industries, agencies and governments; on the stock market, bond market and the economy; on charts for technicians, commodity traders and all kinds of analysts. Many of the services are updated monthly. Address: Standard & Poor's Corporation, 345 Hudson Street, New York, N.Y. 10014.

STOCK: The common stock of a corporation is evidence of ownership of part of the company. It is the riskiest form of investment with the least protection, yet also offers the greatest chance for profit when the enterprise is successful.

Among the widely used terms associated with common stock are:

Clean: This is a company with no particular problems, financial, managerial, legal or regulatory.

Cyclical: These shares follow up-and-down patterns that tend to repeat over a period of months or years.

Declining: A stock whose today's low is tomorrow's high. Despite recurring minor rallies, the basic direction of such a stock is down.

Down: A word synonymous with "declining."

Good: An UP stock in an UP group in an UP market.

Growth: This is the stock of a company with a history of increasing sales, earnings and dividends. Sometimes "growth" stocks are "one-decision" holdings because the only decision is to buy. In past bull markets, many institutions considered such stocks too good to sell—ever. They learned their lesson the hard way. With almost no exceptions, no stock should be held indefinitely.

STOP ORDERS: Generally, *sell* stop orders are used by owners of stock to protect their position or profits. Usually, *buy* stop orders are used by traders wishing to buy, and by short sellers seeking protection for their positions. Both buy and sell stops specify a price. When that price is reached in the marketplace, the stop order becomes a market order and will be executed. Most well-disciplined, professional traders do not put stop orders on the book. They prefer to keep stop levels in their mind—so called "mental stops."

SYNDICATION: This is also known as an *underwriting syndicate.* It refers to a group of brokers who underwrite the selling of a specific number of shares of stock or bonds. Forming a syndicate is a lengthy, complex process. The underwriters may take substantial risks. They buy the stock or bond issue from the issuer at an agreed-upon price; then, in cooperation with another group of selling brokers, they undertake to sell the securities to institutions and individuals at a price high enough to cover costs, expenses and a large commission. The ultimate buyers pay one net price. This is the area of the brokerage business known as "investment banking."

TAKE A POSITION: This means to buy a stock.

TAPE: This refers to the moving ticker tape that reports every trade on the floor of the NYSE and other stock exchanges as it occurs. The consolidated tape shows the symbol of the corporation, the number of shares traded and the price of the transaction.

TECHNICAL ANALYSIS: This is a technique that analyzes the supply-demand relationship through examination of the action of the market or a particular stock. It assumes that the price action of the stock reflects decisions that have taken the fundamentals into account. Technical analysis concentrates on the psychological factors influencing market movements.

TECHNICAL BREAKOUT: The movement of a stock or the market through a significant point of prior resistance. Generally it's a harbinger of higher prices to come and is a favorite buying point for technicians.

THIRTY-POINT WEEK: This is a technical tool based on the historic fact that the maximum gain or loss of the Dow Jones Industrial Average, in a single week, is likely to be 30 points. After such a swing, the market tends to stabilize or reverse direction for a few weeks. But beware of such a guideline in a bear market. The first dip can be followed by another slide of as much as 50 points, also in one week.

TOP TEN WIRE FIRMS: These are the major brokerage organizations with a large number of branch offices across the country: Merrill Lynch, Pierce, Fenner & Smith, Inc.; Bache Halsey Stuart, Inc.; Hutton (E.F.) & Company, Inc.; Dean Witter & Co., Inc.; Reynolds Securities, Inc.; Paine, Webber, Jackson & Curtis, Inc.; Shearson Hayden Stone Inc.; Blyth Eastman Dillon & Co., Inc.; Hornblower & Weeks-Hemphill Noyes; Loeb Rhoades & Co. Also see WIRE FIRM.

TRADING OFF A POSITION: This refers to a strategy whereby shares of a stock are purchased for long-term gains but a portion of the position is traded in and out to profit from short-term swings. A certain percentage of the shares is never traded. In effect, you admit that your long-term objectives may not come to pass, so you take short-term gains when they are available. You leave yourself the option of taking advantage of a big UP move.

TREND: This refers to the basic direction of a stock's movement. It can be short, medium, or long term. One of the major tenets of technical analysis is that a trend is assumed to continue in force until decisively broken.

UPTREND: An illustration of a chart pattern of an uptrending stock. See CHANNEL.

UNDERWRITING: See SYNDICATION.

V FORMATION: This is a chart pattern in which the left line indicates a sharp, quick drop. The bottom is usually accompanied by heavy volume. The right side of the V is formed when the stock reverses and moves up almost as fast as it fell. A breakout of a V is one of the most powerful technical signals.

VOLUME: This refers to the quantity of stock traded. It is measured either in dollars or, more frequently, in the number of shares traded. Volume may also confirm the direction of the price movement.

WARRANTS: These are securities issued by corporations to give the holder the right to purchase a predetermined amount of common stock at a fixed price, usually for a period of several years. They are used in conjunction with a merger or as a "sweetener" with a debt offering to provide the opportunity for the investor to obtain an equity position. Warrants are traded like common stocks and tend to fluctuate in line with the price of the related stock.

WIRE FIRM: A general term applied to larger brokerage houses with numerous branch offices linked by a communications network or wire.